THE EDUCATIONAL RIGHTS OF THE CHURCH AND ELEMENTARY SCHOOLS IN BELGIUM

THE CATHOLIC UNIVERSITY OF AMERICA
CANON LAW STUDIES
No. 336

The Educational Rights of the Church and Elementary Schools in Belgium

A DISSERTATION

SUBMITTED TO THE FACULTY OF THE SCHOOL OF CANON LAW OF THE CATHOLIC UNIVERSITY OF AMERICA IN PARTIAL FULFILLMENT OF THE REQUIREMENTS FOR THE DEGREE OF DOCTOR IN CANON LAW

BY

REV. GOMMAR A. DE PAUW

THE CATHOLIC UNIVERSITY OF AMERICA PRESS
WASHINGTON, D. C.
1953

NIHIL OBSTAT:

EDUARDUS G. ROELKER, S.T.D., J.C.D.

Censor Deputatus

Washingtonii, D. C., die 4 junii, 1952

IMPRIMATUR:

✠PATRICIUS A. O'BOYLE, D.D., LL.D.

Archiepiscopus Washingtoniensis

Washingtonii, D. C., die 4 Junii, 1952

MURRAY & HEISTER
WASHINGTON, D. C.

PRINTED BY
TIMES AND NEWS PUBLISHING CO
GETTYSBURG, PA., U. S. A.

To
the memory
of
MY FATHER
and all the other
PIONEERS
who helped to make
Belgium's Catholic School System
possible

TABLE OF CONTENTS

PAGE

FOREWORD xi

PART ONE

THE CATHOLIC STAND ON THE SCHOOL PROBLEM

CHAPTER

I. PUBLIC ECCLESIASTICAL LAW ON EDUCATION 3

A. Duties and Rights of the Family 4

B. Duties and Rights of the Church 9

1. The Education of Candidates for the Priesthood 10

2. The Religious and Moral Formation of its Members 10

a) The right to demand religious and moral education for all its members 11

b) The right to determine how religious and moral education should be imparted to Catholics 12

c) The right to see that nothing against faith or morals be taught or done within any schools attended by Catholics 15

d) The right to demand that teachers and books be removed because of religion and morality 17

3. The Erection and Administration of Schools 17

C. Duties and Rights of the State 19

1. The Education of All Citizens 20

2. The Training for Certain Civic Duties 21

3. The Promotion of Educational Activities 22

CHAPTER PAGE

II. THE CHRISTIAN PHILOSOPHY OF EDUCATION 24

A. The General Prohibition of non-Catholic Institutions 27

1. The non-Catholic School 27

2. The Neutral School 28

3. The Mixed School 29

B. Justified Attendance at non-Catholic Institutions 31

PART TWO

CATHOLIC ELEMENTARY SCHOOLS IN BELGIUM

III. THE HISTORICAL BACKGROUND—THE DUTCH RULE, 1815-1830 38

A. The School Inspection Law 43

1. The District-Inspector 43

2. The Provincial Committee of Inspectors 44

3. The Central Government 45

B. The Central School Regulations 45

1. The Local Committees of Supervision 45

2. The Authorization of School Books 46

3. The Mixed School 46

IV. THE BELGIAN CONSTITUTION (1831) AND FREEDOM OF INSTRUCTION 48

V. THE COMPROMISE LAW OF 1842 62

VI. THE LAW OF MISFORTUNE (1879) 75

VII. THE RESTORATION LAWS OF 1884 AND 1895 88

CHAPTER PAGE

VIII. THE RECONCILIATION LAW OF 1919 AND ITS PRESENT-DAY APPLICATION 96

A. Compulsory School Attendance 100

B. Various Denominational Schools 102

1. The Independent School 102

2. The Adopted School 103

a) The act of adoption 104

b) The conditions of adoption 106

c) The duration of the adoption 109

3. The Adoptable School 109

C. Public Funds for Denominational Schools 111

D. School Aid to Children 114

E. Religious Instruction in Civil Public Schools 115

CONCLUSIONS 124

BIBLIOGRAPHY 127

ABBREVIATIONS 140

ALPHABETICAL INDEX 141

BIOGRAPHICAL NOTE 147

CANON LAW STUDIES 148

FOREWORD

When in 1945 the University of California published its *United Nations* Series, a non-Catholic Professor and former Faculty-Dean of the Free University of Brussels called Belgium a country of peace and harmony in the field of education, and a successful synthesis of liberty, State-support and State-control. He attributed this good result not only to a growing sense for reality among Catholics toward official civil public schools, but also to the fact that the fierce opponents of Church-education finally bowed to "the self-evident truth that, after all, the religious section of the people is entitled to schools whose spirit is in accordance with their deepest religious feelings." He added, however, that this happy result came only after a long and bitter struggle and as the product of a century-long evolution.[1]

That evolution is exactly the object of this dissertation. The study is restricted, however, to the Belgian civil legislation concerning the elementary schools only, which means the schools now caring for the children from six to fourteen years of age. Not only is this particular field of the School System the most universally practical, but it is also the principal, if not the only one, where finally the Belgians found some harmonious solution for the so-called School Problem, whereas for the higher fields of education, especially in regard to intermediate and technical schools, a satisfactory solution is still being sought.

Various phases of the Belgian school legislation have been treated in historical and political works. The present study, however, considers the matter strictly from the canonical point of view, investigating if and to what extent the Belgian school legislation is in accordance with the doctrine and the law of the Catholic Church without any prejudice to the rights of a modern State. In other words, this study wants to show the history of a modern nation in its effort to render to God the things that are God's in

[1] Grégoire, *Education in Belgium,* in *Belgium,* ed. Goris (Berkeley-Los Angeles: University of California Press, 1945), pp. 226-238.

the field of primary education, without jeopardizing the rights that always should be Caesar's. This particular viewpoint justifies the first part of this study, the Catholic stand on the School Problem, the respective rights of Family, Church, and State towards the education of children, and the Church's claim for truly Catholic schools based upon the Christian philosophy of education.

Although the Belgians as a people and Belgium as a country have a very old background, Belgium as an entirely autonomous and independent political body has existed only since 1830. But, since the history of independent Belgium, and particularly the Belgian Constitution, cannot be fully understood without some acquaintance with previous existing conditions, the second part of this dissertation will open with a brief survey of the school legislation in Belgium under the Dutch Rule (1815-1830) to be followed by a study of the stand of the Belgian Constitution of 1831 towards education in the new-born State.

Step by step the chronological order of this study will lead one from a period of compromises (1831-1846) to gradually growing attacks against the Catholic School System (1846-1878), thence to a bitter "School Fight" (1878-1884). The Restoration-period (1884-1914), interrupted by four years of war, will finally lead to that era of reconciliation that through the law of 1919 and its later applications brought into the Belgian elementary school system the peace and harmony that no attacks from either the Left or the Right and no second World War have been able to disrupt up to our days.

A study of this kind, however, cannot be just an examination of separate law-texts. The work of the legislator can be understood only when looked upon in the framework of its historical milieu. This justifies the importance given in the different chapters of the study to the recapitulation of the historical events that influenced the evolution of the school legislation in particular. The present dissertation is therefore meant as an essay in the form of a canonical-historical study of a composite nature, so as to present a synthetical view by bringing into one consecutive story all the phases of the subject. A study of this type can still find its place among the other contributions covering separate phases of the subject, and which were mostly of the purely historical or polemical type.

He who is acquainted with the world history of the last century knows how the so-called School Problem has been too often in many countries a source of friction between Catholics and non-Catholics, between ecclesiastical and civil authorities, so as to discourage honest people on both sides in their sincere search for mutual understanding and respect for rights. For anyone confronted with similar problems in his own country it may be interesting to watch a country with a Catholic tradition of a thousand years settle the School Problem without hurting the State in the exercise of its rights or hampering other religious denominations in their development.

It is a fact placed beyond dispute, as much as any fact of history can be, that the contribution of Belgium to the development of human civilization has been far more important than one at first sight may be led to expect from a country at present so small in population and territorial extent. The fact that a Belgian was elected President of the first General Assembly of the United Nations was rather a world tribute to a nation than a reward for personal merits.

In regard to the influence exercised by little Belgium upon the glorious history of the great American Republic, various phases of American history are still waiting for their historian to correct the errors earlier historians made in attributing to French and Dutch history events which belong in reality to the history of Belgium.[8] Particularly to the Catholics of America it may be worth while to know more about the Catholic School System in Belgium. This is so, not only on account of the general Belgian influence on the American Church of today, but also on account of the part of Belgium in the building of America's own Catholic educational system, from the time when the very first public school was opened on the soil of the New World by the Flemish Franciscan Friar Pieter van Ghent to the opening of the American

[8] Cf. Bayer, *The Belgians, First Settlers in New York and in the Middle States* (New York: The Devin-Adair Co., 1925); Griffin, *The Contribution of Belgium to the Catholic Church in America, 1523-1857* (Washington, D. C., The Catholic University of America, 1932).

College at Louvain, and finally the opening of the Catholic University of America, which is modeled after the Catholic University of Louvain.[3]

The writer wishes to take this opportunity to pay his grateful and pious respects to the memory of the late Monsignor Professor Doctor Alfons Van Hove, at one time Dean of the Faculty of Canon Law at the Catholic University of Louvain, under whose masterly guidance this study was started, and to the memory of the late Monsignor Professor Doctor Hubert Louis Motry, until yesterday the revered Dean of the Faculty of Canon Law at the Catholic University of America. To his other professors at Louvain and at Washington, D. C., he offers his most sincere thanks for their kind assistance and most helpful direction. His heartfelt thanks are directed to His Excellency, the Most Reverend Charles J. Calewaert, S.T.L.Lov., Bishop of Ghent, and his successor as President of the Diocesan Major Seminary at Ghent, the Very Reverend Canon Leo De Kesel, J.C.L.Lov., for the opportunity of special studies in both Europe and America. To all who in any way contributed to the preparation of this work he offers honest thanks for their interest and aid.

Washington, D. C., May 19, 1952.

---

[3] "America, I fear, will never be able to repay the debt of gratitude which it owes to Flanders; but Catholic Americans will be noble enough to remember at least, how Catholic Belgium has for a number of years educated and supported many of the bravest priests that ever preached the Gospel in America." Bishop William Stang of Fall River, *American Ecclesiastical Review,* XV (1896), 29.

PART ONE

The Catholic Stand on the School Problem

The study of the Catholic position on the School Problem is both juridical and philosophical. Rules concerning institutions of learning can not be separated from the very principles animating that learning. This is the reason why the two official sources of this subject, the Code of Canon Law and the encyclical *Divini Illius Magistri,* while formulating precise rules concerning the schools as such, lay down at the same time general principles affecting Christian education at large.[1]

The present Code of Canon Law includes the whole legislation governing schools in the third book *De Rebus* (Things), fourth part *De Magisterio Ecclesiastico* (The teaching authority of the Church), twenty-second title *De Scholis* (Schools), canons 1372-1383. The title *De Scholis* is intimately connected with the twentieth title *De Divini Verbi Praedicatione* (Preaching of God's word) and the twenty-first title *De Seminariis* (Seminaries). This combination seems most logical to the ecclesiastical legislator, reasoning as follows: One of the means necessary for the Church to attain its end is its Teaching Authority, which is exercised not only through the preaching of the word of God and the formation of the clergy in the seminaries, but also through the school as a normal instrument of teaching.

These canons define first the duties of the faithful, of the parents and those who hold the place of the parents, in reference to the religious training of youth. After this they deal with these topics: the necessity of religious training in any grade of schools; attendance at non-Catholic institutions by Catholic youth; the right of the Church to have its own system of schools, and the

---

[1] Pius XI, litt. encycl. *Divini illius magistri,* 31 dec. 1929—*Acta Apostolicae Sedis, Commentarium Officiale* (Romae, 1909 . . .), XXII (1930) (hereafter cited *AAS*), pp. 49-86.

duty of establishing them whenever the institutions already existing do not fulfill the requirements concerning the religious formation of Catholic youth; finally, the exclusive authority of the Church in matters of religious instruction and morality, and the particular obligations of the local ordinaries and their right of visitation.

In the introduction of his *Divini Illius Magistri* Pius XI delineated the general condition of the times, the agitation around the problem of educational rights and systems, the expressed wishes of numerous bishops and faithful, and his own paternal affection towards youth as so many reasons for his treating of Christian education. After a brief statement on the nature, the importance and the excellence of Christian education, the four parts of the encyclical treat successively of the following points: Who has the mission to educate; who are the subjects to be educated; what of the necessary environment of education: family, educational works, schools; finally, the true nature of Christian education as deduced from its proper end. The Pope concluded by pointing to our Lord Jesus Christ as the Master and Model of all education.

Both the canons and the encyclical for the most part are general in nature. Their particular application, adapted to conditions as they exist in various localities, has been the work of the councils in different ecclesiastical provinces.[2]

The Catholic synthesis of the Public Ecclesiastical Law about education, on the one hand, and the Philosophy of Christian education, on the other, are crystallized in these legal and doctrinal sources.

---

[2] For the Belgian dioceses see: *Acta et Decreta Concilii Provincialis Mechliniensis Quarti (1922)*, Mechliniae, 1923; *Acta et Decreta Concilii Provincialis Mechliniensis Quinti (1937)*, Mechliniae, 1938. Compare with *Acta et Decreta Concilii Plenarii Baltimorensis Tertii (1884)*, Baltimorae, 1886; *Acta et Decreta Concilii Plenarii Americae Latinae (1899)*, Romae, 1902; *Acta et Decreta Primi Concilii Provincialis Torontini (1875)*, Toronto, 1882; *Acta et Decreta Concilii Plenarii Quebecensis (1909)*, Quebeci, 1912.

CHAPTER I

Public Ecclesiastical Law on Education

The whole educational problem consists in the coordination of the respective rights and duties of the three necessary societies into which man is born. Two of these societies, the family and the civil society, belong to the natural order, while the third society, the Church, belongs to the supernatural order.

To mention the supernatural order is of itself sufficient to distinguish us, at the very beginning of this study, from those who take man himself as the ultimate and only norm of morality. All through this dissertation man will be considered as an individual made up of soul and body, with rights and duties and also obligations to cooperate in society with his fellow men under the supreme dominion of Almighty God, Who furthermore in Jesus Christ elevated man's nature in order to bring him to a supernatural end of everlasting happiness.

The two natural societies of which man, a social being, necessarily is a member, are the family and the State, each of which has its own proper structure, rights and duties. The third necessary society into which man is born, when through baptism he receives the divine life of grace, is the Church. Like the family and the State the Church is a necessary society, independent of the will of men in its origin and its structure, and immutable in its essential rights and duties. Like the State the Church is a "perfect society," a juridically self-contained society, having in itself all the means for the attainment of its own end. Unlike the family and the State, the Church is a society of the supernatural order, instituted immediately by Jesus Christ for the supernatural end of man's eternal salvation; and in this supernatural sphere the Church has independent and inviolable rights.[1]

---

[1] Cf. Billot, *Tractatus de Ecclesia Christi* (2 vols., Romae: Apud Aedes Universitatis Gregorianae, 1927), I, 450-466.

Education now belongs to these three societies, in due proportion, corresponding to the coordination of their respective ends in both the natural and the supernatural order. It is the Catholic teaching that all these three societies should have a hand in the work of education. The whole problem, however, reduces itself to the precise clarification of the extent of the power of each society.

A. DUTIES AND RIGHTS OF THE FAMILY

Nature itself tells us that the first and immediate right to educate a child, to determine what moral and social principles shall be impressed upon a child, belongs to the parents. Saint Thomas Aquinas expressed this doctrine in these words: "The father is the principle of generation, of education and discipline and of everything that has to do with the perfecting of human life."[2] The same argument, authoritatively confirmed by the constant teaching of the Church, was appealed to by Pius XI who furthermore insisted upon the direct and inalienable nature of the right of the parents: "The family therefore holds directly from the Creator the mission and hence the right to educate the offspring, a right inalienable because inseparably joined to the strict obligation, a right anterior to any right whatever in civil society and of the State, and therefore inviolable on the part of any power on earth."[3]

Anyone contesting this primary right of the family, so as to maintain that a child belongs to the State before it belongs to the family, puts himself in open contradiction with the common ex-

[2] "Pater est principium et generationis, et educationis, et disciplinae, et omnium quae ad perfectionem vitae pertinent."—*Summa Theologica,* IIa IIae, Q. CII, a. I.

[3] Litt. encycl. *Divini illius magistri,* 31 dec. 1929: "Habet igitur familia proxime a Creatore munus propetereaque ius prolis educandae; quod quidem ius cum abiici nequeat, quia cum gravissimo officio coniunctum, tum cuivis societatis civilis et reipublicae iuri antecedit, eaque de causa nulli in terris potestati illud infringere licet."—*AAS,* XXII (1930), 59. The English translation of the encyclical *Divini illius magistri* used in this study is the revised translation of *The America Press,* based on the translation of the *National Catholic Welfare Conference.*

perience of men, witnessing to the fact that every day children become members of civil society, not directly by themselves, but through the family in which they are born. Before being a citizen, man must exist, and existence does not come from the State but from the parents. And one should not try to restrict the part of the family to a mere bringing into the world, turning the child over almost immediately to what Pope Leo XIII called "the socialistic Providence" of the State.[4] The absolute helplessness of the new-born child and its dependence for many long years on its parents points to them as the natural educators of their children. What good would the gift of life be were it not completed by the education of body and soul, so essential to fitting a person for his responsible place in society?[5]

History has abundantly proved that no State can substitute for parents in a work that requires such a degree of love, patience and self-sacrifice. So long as parents fulfill their task in the religious, moral, intellectual, physical, and civic education of their children, no one has a right to interfere with them. And here one bears in mind not only the State as a possible violator, for one would vindicate this same inviolable right of the family even against any ecclesiastical authority. Of course, the rights of parents to educate their children is not an absolute and despotic right, but one conditioned by God's plan and the divinely established order. This right of parents over their children is derived from their duty to provide, as far as they possibly can, for the complete

---

[4] For further development of these and the following principles, see Leo XIII, litt. encycl. *Rerum novarum,* 15 maii 1891, n. 10—*Codicis Iuris Canonici Fontes,* cura Emī Petri Card. Gasparri editi (9 vols., Romae et Civitate Vaticana: Typis Polyglottis Vaticanis, 1923-1939. Vols. VII-IX ed. cura et studio Emī Iustiniani Card. Serédi), n. 611 (hereafter cited *Fontes*). Cf. also Pius XI, litt. encycl. *Casti connubii,* 31 dec. 1930—*AAS,* XXII (1930), 545; Cappello, *Summa Iuris Publici Ecclesiastici* (2. ed., Romae: apud Aedes Universitatis Gregorianae, 1928), p. 503; Janssens, *Personne et Société. Théories actuelles et Essai doctrinal* (Gembloux: Duculot, 1939); Ottaviani, *Institutiones Iuris Publici Ecclesiastici* (2. ed., 2 vols., Typis Polyglottis Vaticanis, 1935-1936), II, 233.

[5] "Non enim intendit natura solum generationem prolis, sed etiam traductionem et promotionem usque ad perfectum statum hominis, in quantum homo est; qui est virtutis status."—St. Thomas, *Supplementum,* Q. XLI, a. I.

education of their offspring.[6] But so long as they fulfill their duty, they preserve intact their primary and direct right and thus prevent all others from interfering with the child's training.

While past and present history shows how often the State has violated this right conferred by the Creator on the family, it shows at the same time how the Catholic Church has ever scrupulously protected and vigorously defended the rights of all parents. Of course the Church is ever conscious of Christ's injunction to teach all nations, and of the obligation which all men have to practice the one true religion; and therefore the Church will always remind Catholic parents of their duty to have their children baptized and brought up as true Catholics.[7] But on the other hand, the Church realizes that the nature of man calls for opposition to any measure that would destroy or in any essential matter weaken the authority and responsibility of the parents. The Church therefore never consents, save under very special circumstances and with particular cautions, to baptize the children of non-Catholics, or to provide for their education against the will of the parents till such time as the children can decide for themselves and freely choose their Faith.[8] Only as the result of its great respect for the natural rights of the family does the Church willingly take a secondary rôle in this case; in no other case, when the relations between God and man are involved, does the Church act likewise.

It is evident, however, that in the actual conditions of life no

---

[6] *Canon 1113*: "Parentes gravissima obligatione tenentur prolis educationem tum religiosam et moralem, tum physicam et civilem pro viribus curandi, et etiam temporali eorum bono providendi."

[7] *Canon 1372*: "Fideles omnes ita sunt a pueritia instituendi ut non solum nihil eis tradatur quod catholicae religioni morumque honestati adversetur, sed praecipuum institutio religiosa ac moralis locum obtineat.—Non modo parentibus ad normam can. 1113, sed etiam omnibus qui eorum locum tenent, ius et gravissimum officium est curandi liberorum educationem."

[8] *Canon 750*: "Infans infidelium, etiam invitis parentibus, licite baptizatur, cum in eo versatur vitae discrimine, ut prudenter praevideatur moriturus, antequam usum rationis attingat.—Extra mortis periculum, dummodo catholicae educationi cautum sit, licite baptizatur: 1) Si parentes vel tutores, aut saltem unus eorum, consentiant; 2) Si parentes, idest pater, mater, avus, avia, vel tutores desint, aut ius in eum amiserint, vel illud excercere nullo pacto queant."

single family can adequately carry out, in total independence, the complete task of educating its children. Nothing is therefore more natural than that families unite their educational efforts and entrust at least part of the formal education to that social institution which is the school.

Most of the misunderstandings that have created the so-called School Problem would disappear at once if all would only keep in mind the origin and true nature of that social institution. The school has never been and never can be an autonomous institution. The school has no right to teach, except such as is delegated to it by the parents who should have the final word in determining, if not the technical, at least the educational aspect of any School System.[9] For, while partly delegating to others the education of their children, the fundamental responsibility remains with the parents. Even the Catholic Church in justifying its claims for Catholic schools will point to this conception of the school as a subsidiary and complementary institution of the family. Before advancing any dogmatical reasons which non-Catholics could hardly understand, the Church will always present itself as the representative of the families. Against any attempt of State monopoly the Church will defend its schools as the kind of institution freely elected by innumerable parents entrusting their children with confidence to its institutions of education.

Today the word "school" covers any institution which has for its purpose the methodical apprehension of knowledge in different degrees.[10] For the better understanding of the terminology used throughout this dissertation reference should here be made to the more important classifications of schools. Very often the classifications offered by the various authors are more confusing than clari-

---

[9] Pius XI, litt. encycl. *Divini illius magistri,* 31 dec. 1929: ". . . scholae, si, ad historiae fidem, earum originem inspiciamus, natura sua tamquam subsidium ac fere complementum Ecclesiae simul et familiae exstiterunt."—*AAS,* XXII (1930), 76.

[10] Boffa, *Canonical Provisions for Catholic Schools,* The Catholic University of America Canon Law Studies, n. 117 (Washington, D. C.: The Catholic University of America Press, 1939), p. 4; cf. also Vermeersch-Creusen, *Epitome Iuris Canonici* (3 vols., Vol. I, 6. ed., 1937; Vol. II, 6. ed., 1940; Vol. III, 5. ed., 1936, Mechliniae-Romae: Dessain), II, 709.

fying. The logical classifications adverted to in the further development of this study are the following:

By reason of their immediate origin schools are either private or public. *Private schools* are established and governed by private individuals or single families united for the purpose of training their own children. *Public schools,* on the contrary, are founded and governed by a public authority, either ecclesiastical or civil. There are acknowledged then two types of public schools: Ecclesiastical public schools, or Church-schools, and civil public schools, according to whether these public schools come under the control of the Church or of the State. To refer to the official Catholic Schools as if they were private schools is to disregard the fact that these schools are erected by the public authority of a juridically self-contained "perfect society."

On the basis of religion schools are either religious or neutral. In *religious schools* religion is an integral part of the curriculum, whereas in the *neutral schools* religion is just an optional part or no part at all of the program. When a religious school is open only for pupils of one particular belief, the institution is a "denominational or confessional school"; if it is open to pupils of various religious denominations the school should be called a "mixed school," wherein religion is still a compulsory part of the curriculum but taught separately, according to the different beliefs of the pupils.[11]

Looking at the more or less advanced grade of education which they impart, one can distinguish elementary, intermediate, and schools of higher education. Whatever the differences in curriculum and duration might be in various countries, this common general division is equally applicable to all. *Elementary* or *Primary schools* provide for children that fundamental education and

---

[11] *Catholic schools,* of course, are denominational schools. Such are eminently the schools erected and directly controlled by the ecclesiastical authority; these schools form the official Catholic School System. However, the term "Catholic school" has a more extensive meaning in the Code of Canon Law. Besides the Catholic School System, properly so called, the term "Catholic school" includes all other public and private educational institutions which impart a Catholic education under the competent ecclesiastical supervision.

knowledge, which, according to the needs of the times, will either enable them to take their place in society or to develop themselves by further formal studies. ***Intermediate*** or ***Secondary schools*** continue the moral development of the youth, while the more advanced study of letters and sciences prepares him for the study of his chosen profession in a ***School of Higher Learning***.[12]

B. DUTIES AND RIGHTS OF THE CHURCH

Mention has been made of what one likes to refer to as the "historical right" of the Church, which was the first in human history to organize schools, centuries before any similar activity was ever undertaken by the State.[13] In the purely natural order one could explain this as the result of the free delegation, on the part of fathers and mothers, of their own parental authority to the educational institution of their choice. Everyone believing in the personal freedom of the human being should be able to agree with this historical argument. Prescinding from any of its prerogatives as based upon divinely revealed truths that make it a necessary society, one must at least accept the Church as a freely constituted moral person with all the natural rights of any other moral person. Among these rights is that of founding and directing institutions of its own, as long as these institutions observe the just regulations of the State and do not disturb the public order. And when this is concerned, it is history again that shows what the civilized world owes to the Catholic School System.

But, for the Christian the roots of the Church's rights in the field of education lie much deeper, namely in the divine positive

---

[12] On the basis of attendance, elementary schools are either obligatory or optional, according to whether attendance is compulsory by law or not. This distinction is sometimes improperly applied to schools of higher learning or to intermediate schools in so far as some special knowledge or credits are required for the holding of certain offices.

[13] Cf. Lalanne, *Influence des Pères de l'Église sur l'Éducation Publique pendant les Cinq Premiers Siècles de l'Ère Chrétienne* (Paris, 1850); Maitre, *Les Écoles Épiscopales et Monastiques de l'Occident* (Paris, 1866); Marique, *History of Christian Education* (3 vols., New York: Fordham University Press, 1924-1932); Schmid, *Geschichte der Erziehung vom Anfang an bis auf unsere Zeit* (3 vols., Stuttgart, 1884-1892).

law. First of all, the Church is the divinely appointed teacher of all men, educating no longer in the place of the family, but by its own proper right.[14] In the supernatural order it is the Church that through baptism begets the faithful in the order of grace, nurtures them with its sacraments, and educates them with its doctrine.[15] In keeping with these principles of the natural and positive divine law the Church maintains the following rights with regard to the exercise of its native mission: The right to educate its candidates for the clerical life; the right over the religious and moral formation of its members; and the right to erect and govern its own schools.

1. The Education of Candidates for the Priesthood

The Church has the exclusive right to educate its candidates for the clerical life, and consequently the right to found and to direct its minor and major seminaries. This right follows necessarily from the nature of the Church as a completely autonomous society.[16]

2. The Religious and Moral Formation of Its Members

To no one other than to the Church was given divine authority in matters of faith and morals as a means of leading men to salvation. In this spiritual sphere the Church is the supreme, infallible teacher, with the right of universal supervision over individuals, families, and nations.[17]

---

[14] Matthew, XXVIII, 18-20.

[15] Cf. Pius XI, litt. encycl. *Divini illius magistri,* 31 dec. 1929—*AAS,* XXII (1930), 54.

[16] Cf. Canons 1352-1371.—For the claims of some States trying to supervise ecclesiastical studies see Denzinger-Bannwart-Umberg, *Enchiridion Symbolorum, Definitionum, et Declarationum de Rebus Fidei et Morum* (21-23. ed., Friburgi Brisgoviae: Herder & Co., 1937), hereafter cited *Enchiridion.* See especially Pius IX, *Syllabus seu Collectio Errorum modernorum,* prop. 33: "Non pertinet unice ad ecclesiasticam iurisdictionis potestatem proprio ac nativo iure dirigere theologicarum rerum doctrinam," and prop. 46: "Immo in ipsis clericorum seminariis methodus studiorum adhibenda civili auctoritati subiicitur."—Denzinger-Bannwart, *Enchiridion,* nn. 1733, 1746.

[17] Cf. Vatican Council, *Constitutio dogmatica I de Ecclesia Christi,* sess. IV.—Denzinger-Bannwart, *Enchiridion,* n. 1821.

This authority extends over individuals and families as members of the Church by baptism. It is, therefore, the privilege of the Church to determine the duties of parents regarding the religious and moral training of their children. Just as in secular education the Church in its schools acts in the place of the parents, so likewise in the religious and moral education the parents act in the place of the Church in the fulfillment of its mission.

This authority of the Church over the religious and moral formation of its members extends to each and every school attended by Catholics, no matter who founded or directs them. For, Catholic pupils are subjects of the Church which is the only competent authority in all that concerns their religious and moral formation. To deny the Church that direct jurisdiction over its members is to attack its very existence.

In the concrete, this means that the Church claims the right to demand that religious and moral training be given to all its children, and to determine how this training shall be given.

a) The right to demand religious and moral education for all its members.

This right, as the basis of the entire canonical school legislation and the foundation of all Christian education, is expressed in canon 1372, § 1.[18]

By baptism one becomes a member of the Church instituted by Christ for the sanctification and salvation of men. Each member has the right to all the means necessary for the attainment of this end. Among these means a Christian education is pre-eminent.[19] This education, which in the mind of the Church should start from the very early years of childhood, is not just a negative attitude, in the sense that youth be taught nothing against Catholic faith and morals. The Church requires a positive religious and moral

---

[18] "Fideles omnes ita sunt a pueritia instituendi ut non solum nihil eis tradatur quod catholicae religioni morumque honestati adversetur, sed praecipuum institutio religiosa ac moralis locum obtineat."

[19] By its positive law, just a further specification of the natural and positive divine law, the Church cares only for its members. For those outside the Church the natural law will be the only norm in the field of education as in any other field of human conduct.

formation for both mind and will. That formation, according to the Code of Canon Law, must take first place above everything else that may be part of the general education.

This right of a Christian to a complete education affects primarily the family into which he was born, and secondarily the schools as the logical annex of the family. Canon 1372, § 2, clearly specifies that the necessity of providing the Christian education of youth is primarily the duty of the parents or of those who legally occupy their place when the parents are deceased or lack the capacity for imparting the proper education to their children.[20] Referring to canon 1113, the legislator connects this religious and moral training with the other parental duties of providing for the physical and civic education, and caring for the material status of the children.

But, as was mentioned above, the normal "second home" for the child will be the school. Since the faithful have a right to be trained in a positive Christian manner, and since Catholic parents have the duty to provide their children with such an education, canon 1373 most logically asserts that in every school a progressive religious training should be provided, adapted to the age, the development of the mind, and the practical needs of the pupils.[21]

b) The right to determine how religious and moral education should be imparted to Catholics.

The unique authority of the Church as the divinely appointed teacher of faith and morals does not stop with the theoretical declaration of some general principles; it extends right to the practical organization of the religious and moral training of its members. Because of its divine right over the religious formation of its children in schools, the Church claims the right to approve the teachers and textbooks used in this work, and to visit and

---

[20] "Non modo parentibus ad normam can. 1113, sed etiam omnibus qui eorum locum tenent, ius et gravissimum officium est curandi christianam liberorum educationem."

[21] "In qualibet elementaria schola, pueris pro eorum aetate tradenda est institutio religiosa.—Iuventus, quae medias vel superiores scholas frequentat, pleniore religionis doctrina excolatur, et locorum Ordinarii curent ut id fiat per sacerdotes zelo et doctrina praestantes."

inspect any and all schools in what pertains to this religious and moral formation.[22] This authority of the Church belongs *in concreto* to the appropriate superior legally constituted according to the degrees of hierarchical jurisdiction. In the first place it belongs to the Pope, who, since the days of Peter, has supreme and infallible authority in matters of faith and morals, and jurisdiction over the universal Church. By the same divine authority the bishops, in union with the Roman Pontiff, are constituted judges in faith and morals in their respective dioceses.[23]

a'. The right at least to approve, if not to appoint, teachers and textbooks to be used in the teaching of the Catholic religion.

In Catholic schools properly so called there is no difficulty in this regard. The complete direction of these schools is under the control of the proper ecclesiastical authority which appoints duly qualified teachers. The case, however, is different for both private and civil public schools.

Private schools for Catholic children, as any other school, must provide the necessary religious training. Since in this particular type of school the natural link between family and school is most evident, the question can be asked: Does the Church have any direct authority over these teachers who are the immediate representatives of the parental authority? The answer is certainly affirmative. When the parents themselves are subject to the Church in the religious and moral education of their children, is this *a fortiori* true for teachers whose only rights are delegated ones. The Church may not have the right to appoint teachers of religion in private schools, but the Church has certainly and in all circumstances the right and the duty to demand its positive approbation for all teachers of the Catholic religion. In this, one can not

---

[22] *Canon 1381*: "Religiosa iuventutis institutio in scholis quibuslibet auctoritati et inspectioni Ecclesiae subiicitur.—. . . Eisdem [Ordinariis locorum] ius est approbandi religionis magistros et libros. . . ."

Canon 1382: "Ordinarii locorum sive ipsi per se sive per alios possunt quoque scholas quaslibet . . . in iis quae religiosam et moralem institutionem spectant, visitare. . . ."

[23] Concilium Tridentinum, sess. XXIII, *de sacramento ordinis, c. 4, De ecclesiastica hierarchia et ordinatione.*—Denzinger-Bannwart, *Enchiridion*, n. 960.

follow authors who exclude this right of the Church in cases wherein "it may be presumed that these teachers have the necessary qualifications."[24] When the "safe instruction of the faithful" is involved, the qualifications of the teachers are not to be "presumed" but should be investigated. Furthermore, teaching in a school can no longer be called "private religious instruction." Finally, these teachers of religion do not represent the proper authority of the parents, which is capable of direct delegation. As teachers of religion and morals the parents themselves are only the representatives of the Church which, therefore, alone has the right at least to approve, if not to appoint, those who carry on its own work of teaching religion.

In civil public schools also the Church requires Catholic religious training for Catholic pupils. The fact that many States do not recognize this right of the Church over its members does not affect the solid basis of this right. But the Church is realistic enough to admit that, even when the civil authorities are most cooperative, the practical organization of religious teaching may be dictated by circumstances in proportion to the number of Catholics and of schools in certain communities. A teacher of religion may be required to give religious training solely, while another teacher may be appointed for other subjects besides. What rights does the Church claim in either case?

In both cases the Church considers a person when teaching the Catholic religion in a school as sharing in its own public teaching office for which one must receive a formal ecclesiastical authorization. This authorization will take the form of either the nomination of the person to teach religion alone, or the simple approval of the person who is required by the school authorities to teach other subjects also. The reason for this intervention of the Church can hardly be questioned by one who recognizes the Church as the competent authority for the imparting of religious instruction to its own members.

But not only the qualifications of the teachers is subject to the

---

[24] Boffa, *Canonical Provisions for Catholic Schools,* p. 167, referring to Cavagnis, *Institutiones Iuris Publici Ecclesiastici* (3 vols., 4. ed., Romae, 1906), III, 29.

authority of the Church. The Church also claims the right to approve the books to be used in the courses of religion. If it is within the Church's province to teach faith and morals, it is but logical for the same Church to control the means used for this teaching, be it the official catechism or be they other books, such as the Bible, Church histories, apologetical works, and the like.

b'. The right to visit and to inspect any and all schools in what concerns the religious and moral formation of Catholic youth.

This right of inspection is but one particular expression of the Church's authority in this matter. Authority would be purely hypothetical without the right of inspection. And since no information is more reliable than that collected by means of a personal visitation, canon 1382 confirms the right of local ordinaries to visit all schools within their territorial jurisdiction and to examine them in what concerns the religious and moral formation of Catholic youth. Despite *de facto* contrary situations in many modern countries, the Church, faithful to its divine mission, will never cease to claim this right over all schools attended by Catholics. No matter what the status of these schools may be as far as their establishment and management is concerned, the Church alone is the divinely appointed authority in what has to do with the religious and moral formation of its members. Neither central nor local governments should oppose this right by laying down restrictions or conditions against a jurisdiction that in its own field is unlimited.

c) The right to see that nothing against faith or morals be taught or done within any schools attended by Catholics.[25]

Whereas the above mentioned rights, namely to demand and to determine the religious and moral training, belong immediately in the spiritual sphere wherein the Church has an independent, proper, direct, and absolute authority, this new right of the Church

---

[25] *Canon 1381*, § *2*: "Ordinariis locorum ius et officium est vigilandi ne in quibusvis scholis sui territorii quidnam contra fidem vel bonos mores tradatur aut fiat."

can only be regarded as an indirect right, affecting temporal things such as the curriculum and the discipline of the schools. On account, however, of the more or less close connection between temporal goods and supernatural values, the Church claims a certain indirect authority over the temporal sphere of life also.

This principle applies particularly to the matters touching religion and morals in the schools where it is the Church's preventive duty to see that the teaching of the secular sciences be not in opposition to the revealed doctrine, and that the general educational system of the school be not lacking in conformity to the moral standards of Christianity.

Again, the fact that many modern States prevent the Church from carrying out its work of vigilance over its own children in the civil public schools neither dispenses the Church from its duty, nor deprives it of its right to do so. Possessing rights and authority is one thing, their practical application is another. Pius XI illustrated the same doctrine when he wrote: "It is the inalienable right as well as the indispensable duty of the Church, to watch over the entire education of her children, in all institutions, public or private, not merely in regard to religious instruction there given, but in regard to every other branch of learning and every regulation insofar as religion and morality are concerned. Nor should the exercise of this right be considered undue interference, but rather maternal care on the part of the Church in protecting her children from the grave danger of all kinds of doctrinal and moral evil. Moreover this watchfulness of the Church not merely can create no real inconvenience, but must on the contrary confer valuable assistance in the right ordering and well-being of families and of civil society; for it keeps far away from youth the moral poison which at that inexperienced and changeable age more easily penetrates the mind and more rapidly spreads its baneful effects."[26]

---

[26] Litt. encycl. *Divini illius magistri*, 31 dec. 1929: "Est praeterea Ecclesiae et ius, quod abdicare, et officium, quod deserere nequit, pro tota vigilandi educatione, qualiscumque filiis suis, scilicet fidelibus, in institutis vel publicis vel privatis impertitur, non modo quod attinet ad religiosam, quae ibidem tradatur, doctrinam, sed etiam quod ad quamlibet aliam disciplinam rerumve

d) The right to demand that teachers and books be removed because of religion and morality.[27]

Here again the Church is claiming an indirect right, perfectly, however, in conformity with its mission of saving souls. Defending the faith and safeguarding the morality of its young members, the Church is entitled to demand that unfit teachers or dangerous books be removed because of their attitude towards religion and morality. Here, too, the Church's right extends to every school attended by Catholics. The practical execution of this principle will, of course, be different according to circumstances of place and time.[28]

3. The Erection and Administration of Schools

The right of the Church to found and to govern its own schools is only a consequence of its right to teach, schools being among the ordinary means of achieving education.[29] However, when private schools or civil public schools correspond with the above explained prescriptions of Canon Law, particularly of canon 1373, there is no danger to faith and morals for Catholic pupils attending them. In this case neither the natural nor the positive divine law require that the Church use its right to found its own

---

ordinationem, quatenus cum religione morumque praeceptis aliquid habeant necessitudinis.

"Atque Ecclesia, ius eiusmodi exercendo, non se in aliena perperam immiscere videatur, immo potius materna quadam, eademque insigni, providentia consulere, ut filios suos ab gravi tueatur incolumes periculo omne virus imbibendi, quod doctrinae integritatem morumque sanctitudinem inficiat. Quae quidem Ecclesiae vigilantia, ut nullum potest verum parere incommodum, sic nequit ad familiarum et Civitatis ordinem prosperitatemque non efficaciter conducere, cum ab adolescentibus illam arceat pestem, quae in aetatulam imperitam ac mobilem facilius ingruere et celerius in ipsum vivendi morem permanare solet."—*AAS,* XXII (1930), 56.

[27] Canon 1381, § 2: "[Ordinariis locorum ius est] religionis morumque causa, exigendi ut tum magistri tum libri removeantur."

[28] Cf. Doyle, *Education in Recent Constitutions and Concordats* (Washington, D. C.: The Catholic University of America, 1933), pp. 92-124. Compare with Dareste, *Les Constitutions modernes* (4. ed., Paris, 1928).

[29] *Canon 1375*: "Ecclesiae est ius scholas cuiusvis disciplinae non solum elementarias, sed etiam medias et superiores condendi."

schools. Never has the Church claimed a monopoly in education. On the contrary, the Church welcomes as a great relief from grave material and financial worries any private or civil public school system wherein Catholic children receive an education corresponding to the divine and ecclesiastical law. But, when existing schools do not guarantee the proper religious and moral training of Catholic youth, then a Catholic School System, properly so called, becomes a necessity.[30] For elementary and intermediate schools the law makes it an obligation (*curandum est*); for the foundation of Catholic universities the ecclesiastical legislator expresses only a wish (*optandum*), for the implementing of which the local ordinaries will be the judges.

The Code puts this obligation primarily upon local ordinaries, particularly upon residential bishops, who are the proper and first pastors responsible for the care of souls.[31] But this obligation of establishing Catholic schools affects also in differing degrees the other members of the Church, both priests and lay people, in the measure of their responsibility for carrying out the mission of their Church. And in a special enactment the Church points out that the obligation of erecting, and consequently, of supporting Catholic schools does not rest upon parents only, but upon all the faithful, who are bound in conscience to do their part in maintaining their schools to the best of their abilities.[32] In his encyclical on Christian education Pius XI commented on this obligation with these words: "Catholics will never feel, whatever may have been the sacrifices already made, that they have done enough for the support and the defense of their schools, and for the securing of laws that will do them justice. For whatever Catholics do in promoting and defending the Catholic school for their children

[30] *Canon 1379, §§ 1-2*: "Si scholae catholicae ad normam can. 1373 sive elementariae sive mediae desint, curandum, praesertim a locorum Ordinariis, ut condantur.—Itemque si publicae studiorum Universitates doctrina sensuque catholico imbutae non sint, optandum ut in natione vel regione Universitas catholica condatur."

[31] *Canon 334, § 1*: "Episcopi residentiales sunt ordinarii et immediati pastores in dioecesibus sibi commissis."

[32] *Canon 1379, § 3*: "Fideles ne omittant adiutricem operam pro viribus conferre in catholicas scholas condendas et sustentandas."

is a genuinely religious work, and, therefore, an important task of Catholic Action. For this reason the associations which in various countries are so zealously engaged in this work of prime necessity, are especially dear to our paternal heart and are deserving of every commendation."[33]

C. DUTIES AND RIGHTS OF THE STATE

In no circumstances has the Church ever denied the civil power its natural rights in the education of its citizens. Pius XI merely confirmed an acknowledged doctrine when he spoke of "true and just rights of the State in the education of its citizens . . . rights conferred upon civil society by the Author of nature Himself, not by title of fatherhood, as in the case of the Church and the family, but in virtue of the authority which it possesses to promote the common temporal welfare, which is precisely the purpose of its existence."[34]

Common sense and the experience of history prove that the general temporal welfare can only be procured when civil authority respects the prior rights of individuals, of families, and of the Church. In the particular field of education, therefore, the rôle of the State must be entirely secondary, for the natural law desig-

---

[33] Litt. encycl. *Divini illius magistri,* 31 dec. 1929: ". . . homines catholici numquam satis, vel per maximas molestias, in eo elaborabunt ut scholas suas tueantur incolumes et iustae de libera adolescentium institutione leges auspicato condantur.

"Quicquid autem ad scholam catholicam in filiorum suorum usum provehendam ac tuendam a christifidelibus agitur, opus religionis sine ulla dubitatione est, propptereaque potissimum "Actionis Catholicae" munus; ita ut paterno animo Nostro pergratae sint, sintque praecipuis laudibus dignae sodalitates illae omnes, quae multifariam in opus tam necessarium peculiari modo ac studiosissime incumbunt."—*AAS,* XXII (1930), 79. Cf. Civardi, *A Manual of Catholic Action* (New York: Sheed & Ward, 1936).

[34] Litt. encycl. *Divini illius magistri,* 31 dec. 1929—*AAS,* XXII (1930), 62; cf. also litt. encycl. *Non abbiamo bisogno,* 29 iun. 1931—*AAS,* XXIII (1931), 303; Bender, *Kerk en Staat* (Kortrijk: Zonnewende, 1938); Chénon, *Histoire des Rapports de l'Église et de l'État du Ier au XXe Siècle* (Paris, 1913); Lecler, *L'Église et la Souveraineté de l'État* (Paris: Ed. Flammarion, 1946; Moulart, *L'Église et l'État, ou les Deux Puissances* (Louvain: Van Linthout, 1895).

nates the parents as the first educators of their children, while the positive divine law has made the Church the teacher of all men in whatever concerns faith and morals. Though secondary, the place of civil authority is nonetheless real because with respect to the safeguarding of the common temporal welfare the State has specific rights and duties: the right to see that education reaches all future citizens; the right to reserve to itself the training for certain civic duties; the right to encourage and to supplement, if necessary, the educational activity of the family and of the Church.

1. The Education of All Citizens

This right of the State extends not only to the removal of public impediments that may stand in the way of education; not only to the general promotion of knowledge by institutions like libraries, museums and the like; it extends also to the protection of the rights of the child itself when parents would fail in their obligations. Known indeed are cases wherein parental neglect becomes a real danger to society, when children, through lack of education, become potential criminals menacing the social order. By compelling such parents to perform their duty the civil authority is only protecting the children's natural right and defending its own existence. When parents fail in this duty, the State can even go so far as to take the children away from their unworthy parents and itself send them to a school where the proper religious, moral, and general education will be imparted.

But these are exceptional cases of serious neglect. Outside such cases, does the State have a general right to restrict the parents' control over the education of their children so as, for instance, to justify the compulsory instruction laws of our modern countries? In other words, should such legislation be called an unjust encroachment upon the natural rights of parents, or merely an inevitable necessity for the modern State as a minimum required for the normal education of its future citizens? The adoption of the latter supplies the right answer, with this essential condition, however, that the State approves of or provides that type of school that parents rightly demand. That means, for Catholic parents, schools in accord with the divine and ecclesiastical law, as was explained before, and providing at the same time the intellectual and civic education that the State rightly may expect from any educational institution. Only on this condition can the Church agree with the principle of a compulsory school attendance system.[35] But no Catholic can ever approve of the modern State ordering all parents to send their children to school, and then providing at the public expense single-type-schools set up without regard to the religious and moral education as wished by the parents.

2. The Training for Certain Civic Duties

This right is evident for the training of military officers and of diplomatic and other officials who are, as it were, the immediate representatives of the State itself. The control of their training in special State schools belongs to the State just as the training of the clergy belongs to that other autonomous society, the Church. But the same can not be said about other professions such as those of lawyers, physicians, teachers in civil public schools, and government employees, or other professions that in an indirect way can still be called public professions. Of course, in these cases too the State is entitled to see to the professional fitness of the candidates for such positions. But by what right could a government deprive a qualified candidate of a certain public position, in

---

[35] This conditional assent to the principle of legal coercion is found again in the encyclical on Christian education, *Divini illius magistri,* 31 dec. 1929, where Pius XI, without actually mentioning compulsory education wrote: "Praecipere Civitas potest ac proinde curare ut cives omnes cum civilia et nationalia iura perdiscant, tum a scientia, doctrina morum physicisque ludis instructi sint quantum decet atque hisce nostris temporibus commune bonum reapse postulat. Verumtamen plane liquet, eo Civitatem officio teneri, ut, in publica privataque educatione omnibus his modis provehenda, non solum nativa Ecclesiae et familiae iura christiane educandi vereatur, sed etiam iustitiae quae suum cuique tribuit parere. Itaque nefas est, Civitatem educationis institutionisque causam ita ad se redigere totam, ut familiae, contra christianae conscientiae officia vel contra quam legitime malint, physice aut moraliter ad Civitatis ipsius scholas liberos suos mittere cogantur."—*AAS,* XXII (1930), 63-64.

view of his attendance at an educational institution that was founded on a particular religion or moral philosophy?

3. The Promotion of Educational Activities

If the co-operation between families and Church results in the successful and complete education of the young citizens, the State should express its appreciation for this achievement of fundamental importance to the well-being of the human society. It should, moreover, encourage the continuation of that work, by granting facilities similar to those already given to the public schools under its direct control. In other words, the State should grant to successful private or Church institutions of learning a proper portion of the public money set aside for education. This is the very question that has upset the relations between Church and State in so many places: the question of public funds for denominational schools.[36]

And yet, for one who admits a duty of distributive justice for any well-ordered civil society, nothing seems more natural than that public funds be used to the advantage of all those who contributed them. Not only are the natural rights of parents jeopardized, but also the elementary sense of "equal justice for all" is shocked in consequence of the situation that confronts Catholics in many countries supposedly governed by the people and for the people: Catholic citizens, forced to pay taxes for a civil public School System which in conscience they can not accept for their own children, and, at the same time, forced to carry all by themselves the financial burden of the schools which their conscience dictates as the institutions wherein their children are also to be trained as citizens second to none.

If, for some reason or other, the combined activity of families and the Church falls short of providing a complete system of public education, then, of course, the State has the duty and the right to found and organize its own School System in addition to existing private or denominational schools. But even then, in

---

[36] Cf. Gabel, *Public Funds for Church and Private Schools* (Washington, D. C.: The Catholic University of America Press, 1937).

its own School System, the rôle of the State must always remain secondary, because to the parents and to the Church, and not to the State, was given the primary right and the original mission to teach and educate.

For this reason the management of such schools should be handed over to local civil authorities as being more closely connected with the parents than any central governmental authorities.

For the same reason these civil public schools should be truly religious schools if practically all the parents of the children in attendance so desired. If all children belong to the same religion, these civil public schools should then be, if not *de iure,* at least *de facto,* denominational schools, whether it be Catholic, Protestant, Jewish, Moslem, or any other type of organized religion. In most other cases the "mixed school" will be the answer to the justified wishes of the parents. If, however, circumstances would force the civil authorities to keep its public schools "neutral" instead of religious, it would then be the irksome task for the controlling body of these schools to keep them really as neutral as possible, by not hurting any pupil's religious or philosophical conviction; by not scandalizing any conscience; by recognizing the above explained rights of the Church over the education of its members; by including in its educational system at least some basic moral principles without which no education is ever possible, not supplanting, however, positive religion with a so-called lay-morality.

To what extent officially called "neutral schools" can ever reach this theoretical ideal of neutrality is a separate question. It will be touched upon in the following chapter on the philosophy of Christian education.

CHAPTER II

The Christian Philosophy of Education

In the non-Catholic world of today there is a general tendency to regard the work of education as something separate from religion. Practically all non-Catholic writers on education do not admit the transcendental and primary right of the parents over the education of their children. Far less do they recognize the supernatural character of the Church and its claims to the highest right in religious and moral formation of its members.

Suffice it to say that there will always be a chasm dividing those who believe in God as the ultimate norm of morality for man created for a supernatural end, and those who look upon man as another temporary worker experimenting on this globe in order to get the best and the most out of this short existence.

But, since it can not be denied that man does not live to himself alone, but as a member of society, the non-Catholic also must recognize the need for some sort of education. This education, however, should aim no longer at the final attainment of the supernatural end, but only at the practical training of the members of this temporal society.[1] The school, according to their theories, should be an institution controlled and directed by the State, solely for the formation of intelligent citizens.[2]

But, even an education aimed exclusively at making the child a good citizen still supposes true character-training and some moral formation. On the one hand the traditional Catholic doctrine is very simple, namely that religion and morality go together

---

[1] "Nicht für die Zwecke des Himmels und für übernatürliche Dinge, sondern für ihre irdischen Aufgaben und als Mitglieder der menschlichen Gesellschaft sollen die Kinder erzogen werden."—Schulz, *Die Schulreform der Sozialdemokratie* (2. ed., Berlin, 1919), p. 89.

[2] Cf. Dunning, *History of Political Theories from Rousseau to Spencer* (New York: The Macmillan Company, 1926), pp. 442-446. Compare with De Hovre, *Philosophy and Education* (New York: Benziger, 1931).

and can not successfully be separated in education. On the other hand, the non-Catholic theories are complicated and inconsistent when trying to determine the character and the morality that go to make the good citizen. If there are no absolute moral standards, and if both the Church and the family are to be excluded from determining the character-formation of the child, who then shall say what sort of moral code the young citizen is to be given? Some writers contend that "experts" should lay down some general norms in accordance with the traditional mores of the country; others call upon the State for the setting up of a code of morals; still others open the door for a veritable educational anarchy by making the children the final authority in their own education, permitting them to "adapt" the accepted mores to their own personal and social needs.[3]

These views, as entertained by non-Catholic educators, are diametrically opposed to the Catholic conception of education. Though directed primarily to the supernatural end of forming "Christ Himself in those regenerated by baptism," Catholic education has never renounced the natural goal of human education, namely the formation of useful citizens. As Pius XI again stated it: "This fact is proved by the whole history of Christianity and its institutions, which is nothing else but the history of true civilization and progress up to the present day."[4] A mere objective study of this history would bring the proper answer to those who still keep asking if a truly Catholic education is not inimical to social progress and temporal prosperity.

But the proper and direct end of Christian education will always be the formation of the true Christian, "the supernatural man who thinks, judges and acts constantly and consistently in accordance with right reason illumined by the supernatural light

---

[3] Cf. Dewey, *Democracy and Education* (New York: The Macmillan Company, 1916), p. 348.

[4] Litt. encycl. *Divini illius magistri,* 31 dec. 1929: "Id profecto tota comprobat christianae religionis eiusque institutorum historia—quacum historia germani civilis cultus humanarumque progressionum, ad nostros usque dies, omnino cohaeret. . . ."—*AAS,* XXII (1930), 84.

of the example and teaching of Christ; in other words, to use the current term, the true and finished man of character."[5]

This education is not just the development of the intellect, but also, if not more, the training of the will. Training of the will means directing youth to do good and avoid evil, in accordance with the principles of the natural law. Daily experience and the facts of a long human history confirm the Church's view that moral principles that are not based on religion will, after some time, lose their force. Education implies a direct training of the will. The ideal held up must be a moral system which presupposes religion as its requisite and adequate foundation. Only religion teaches the meaning of man's obligations before God, the only lasting sanction for the keeping of the moral order, so much so that, once the tie of religion is broken, there can be no true concept of morality.[6]

While insisting on the necessity of religion in education, the Church has primarily in mind the Catholic education of its own children. If religion is necessary in every branch of education, and consequently in the school, then for Catholic children that religion will be the Catholic one to provide them with a true Christian education. It is self-evident that, therefore, only Catholic schools can be the rule for Catholics, even in a nation where there are different religious beliefs.

By a Catholic school, however, is understood any school, regardless of its origin or management, that complies with the principles set down by the Church. As was explained above, the Church does not claim the monopoly of erecting and governing schools, not even for its own members. What the Church demands for Catholics are schools wherein the Catholic spirit actuates teachers and pupils alike, and pervades the entire educational system.[7]

---

[5] Pius XI, litt. encycl. *Divini illius magistri,* 31 dec. 1929: ". . . supernaturalis homo, qui sentit, iudicat, constanter sibique congruenter operatur, ad rectam rationem, exemplis doctrinaque Iesu Christi supernaturaliter collustratam: scilicet, homo germana animi firmitate insignis."—*AAS*, XXII (1930), 83.

[6] Cf. Leo XIII, ep. encycl. *Nobilissima,* 8 febr. 1884, n. 4—*Fontes,* n. 590; litt. encycl. *Sapientiae,* 10 ian. 1890, nn. 16, 20—*Fontes,* n. 605; Cappello, *Summa Iuris Publici Ecclesiastici,* pp. 502-503.

[7] Cf. Pius XI, litt. encycl. *Divini illius magistri,* 31 dec. 1929—*AAS,* XXII (1930), 80-81.

Only when this spirit is missing in existing schools will the Church demand the erection of its own schools, making it obligatory upon parents to send their children to such. Since no other than Catholic schools can guarantee a Catholic education, it is most easy to understand why the Church forbids its members to attend non-Catholic institutions, unless some very special circumstances would justify an exception.[8] Two parts can be distinguished in canon 1374: the first lays down a general prohibition, the second establishes with certain restrictions and measures a possible exception.

A. THE GENERAL PROHIBITION OF NON-CATHOLIC INSTITUTIONS

This rule, by most canonists applied to schools of every rank and grade, is clarified by the legislator who mentions specifically the different schools that are forbidden: the non-Catholic, the neutral, and the mixed schools.[9]

1. The non-Catholic School

Under this term are comprehended the anti-Catholic schools and the non-Catholic denominational schools. By anti-Catholic schools we mean those institutions the principles of which are directly and hostilely opposed to Catholic principles. Under this category we would like to include particularly the so-called "lay-school." Such a school and a "neutral school" are two different things. While neutrality means the absence of any particular preference in the presence of different religious philosophies, the lay-system implies taking a stand against all of them. For the modern lay-philosopher each organized religion is an enemy to be destroyed, an obstacle to be removed from the road to progress and civilization. That many times "lay" and "neutral" have been con-

---

[8] *Canon 1374*: "Pueri catholici scholas acatholicas, neutras, mixtas, quae nempe etiam acatholicis patent, ne frequentent. Solius autem Ordinarii loci est discernere, ad normam instructionum Sedis Apostolicae, in quibus rerum adiunctis et quibus adhibitis cautelis, ut periculum perversionis vitetur, tolerari possit ut eae scholae celebrentur."

[9] For the complete interpretation of this canon see Boffa, *Canonical Provisions for Catholic Schools,* pp. 107-121, where also other commentaries are discussed.

sidered as interchangeable may have some foundation in reality, as often so-called neutral schools turned out to be nothing but anti-religious institutions.[10]

The non-Catholic schools also included in this prohibition are all denominational institutions aimed at educating their pupils on the basis of what, according to Catholic teaching, is a heretical, a schismatical or a pagan religion.

This stand of the Church, forbidding both anti-Catholic and non-Catholic denominational schools, is but a logical deriving from the fact that Christ founded only one Church, and that only the Catholic Church has within itself irrefutable evidences of this divine origin.[11]

2. *The Neutral School*

Neutral are called those schools in which, supposedly out of respect for all philosophical or religious systems, religion is just an optional part, or no part at all, of the curriculum.

Originated and positively intended by Freemasonry to be a weapon against any organized religion, and conducted by teachers whose "neutrality" is an educational impossibility, these theoretical neutral schools are bound to become centers of at least religious indifferentism.[12]

Teachers can not always set aside their religious or non-religious way of thinking, and will necessarily influence the minds of their pupils with either truth or error. "One must be a novice in human affairs," wrote the Holy Office, "if one does not see the dangers

---

[10] Some, as Auxiliary Bishop Bornet of Lyon, go even further, calling the lay-school not only an anti-Catholic institution, but simply another kind of denominational school, based this time upon a negative religion. Cf. Bornet, *La Position de l'Église en face du Problème de l'École* (Paris: Flammarion, 1943), pp. 98-99.

[11] Vatican Council, Sess. III, *Constitutio dogmatica de fide catholica,* cap. 3: "Ad solam enim catholicam Ecclesiam ea pertinent omnia, quae ad evidentiam fidei christianae credibilitatem tam multa et tam mira divinitus sunt disposita."—Denzinger-Bannwart, *Enchiridion,* n. 1794.

[12] Cf. Leo XIII, ep. encycl. *Nobilissima,* 8 febr. 1884, n. 4—*Fontes,* n. 590; Pius XI, litt. encycl. *Divini illius magistri,* 31 dec. 1929—*AAS,* XXII (1930), 76-77.

which teachers not of the fold bring into the class-room. In season and out of season they take every possible occasion to circumvent the simplicity of youth and to bend it, so to speak, into conformity with their tenets; their schemes becoming even more efficacious as they are secret."[13] And even if total abstraction from religious and moral values were possible, it would only result in the imparting of a very incomplete education, since a curriculum devoid of all religious instruction would deprive the pupils of the training most necessary for life.[14]

3. The Mixed School

The Church rejects also this type of school where the pupils are provided with separate religious instruction according to their different beliefs, but receive other lessons in common.

Here the danger to the faith of Catholics lies in the spirit of indifferentism, which logically flows from recognition of all faiths as being of equal worth and relative value. Besides, if religion is divorced from the rest of the program and taught as something optional, the young mind most logically will think very little of the practical value of religious doctrine.[15]

And let it not be said that national unity and necessary civic education call for neutral or mixed schools where Catholic youth will mingle with others of every or no faith, just as will happen in later life. Apart from the school as the place of formal education, there are indeed many other opportunities left for Catholics to make contacts that will help them to know and respect their fellow-citizens. Besides, looking objectively at the Catholic edu-

---

[13] S.C.S. Off., instr. 21 mart. 1866: ". . . novus profecto in humanis rebus sit oportet qui non sentiat etiam in eiusmodi scholis aditum haereticis magistris undequaque aperiri, ut puerilem simplicitatem opportune et importune, data et non data occasione circumveniat, et in laqueos inducat, cuius quo magis inopinae atque occultae sunt artes, eo magis sunt ad perdendum efficaces."—*Fontes,* n. 992.

[14] Cf. S.C.S. Off., instr. (ad Ep. Stat. Foeder. Americae Septentrion), 24 nov. 1875—*Fontes,* n. 1046.

[15] For the question of attendance at Catholic institutions by non-Catholics, as permitted by the Church in exceptional cases, see Boffa, *Canonical Provisions for Catholic Schools,* pp. 121-126.

cational system, the impartial observer will note that it engenders a positive respect for the opinions of others. And where the civic education through Catholic schools is questioned, it may be sufficient to refer to their honor-rolls which proudly display the names of former pupils who made the supreme sacrifice in defending the flag of their country and the ideals it stands for.

Furthermore, Catholics can never admit the attitude of naturalistic liberalism espoused by those who appeal to respect for human liberty in order to prevent the teaching of religion before a certain age, and only after that give the child a free choice between several beliefs and irreligion. Not only theological but also philosophical and pedagogical reasons are the basis of the Church's traditional demand that Catholic youth from its earliest years be educated in the one true faith.[16]

It must be clear, then, that all these reasons justifying the stand of the Church in prohibiting Catholics from attendance at non-Catholic schools are not mere expressions of a disciplinary Church law. One is confronted here with natural and positive divine law forbidding a Catholic to place himself in the occasion of losing his faith, the greatest gift of God to the soul. The positive ecclesiastical law in this matter merely corroborates the divine law.[17]

This positive ecclesiastical legislation, however, is given for the common good in view of a general danger. Such legislation, made for the purpose of safeguarding the faithful against a common danger, is always binding, even though in a particular case there is no danger at all.[18] In other words, the evaluation of the gravity

---

[16] Cf. Boffa, *op. cit.,* pp. 80-82.

[17] Many documents of the Holy See, confirming the common experience, prove that this danger to faith and morals may exist not only in elementary and intermediate schools, but also, if not more, in institutions of higher learning. As to elementary and intermediate schools, especially the civil public schools in the U. S. A., see Instruction of the Holy Office, 24 Nov. 1875—*Fontes,* n. 1046; as to institutions of higher learning, see S.C. Prop. Fid., 7 Apr., 1860—*Fontes,* n. 4649, and earlier documents there cited; also S.C. Prop. Fid., 6 Aug., 1867—*Fontes,* n. 4868.

[18] *Canon 21*: "Leges latae ad praecavendum periculum generale, urgent, etiamsi in casu particulari periculum non adsit." Cf. Van Hove, *Commentarium Lovaniense in Codicem Iuris Canonici,* Vol. I, Tom. II, *De Legibus Ecclesiasticis* (Mechliniae-Romae: Dessain, 1930), nn. 332-337.

of the danger is no longer a matter for the faithful to decide; it is the ecclesiastical authority itself that will determine possible exceptions to the general prohibition.

B. JUSTIFIED ATTENDANCE AT NON-CATHOLIC INSTITUTIONS

Adding to the obligation of the natural law, canon 1374 states that it is for the local ordinary, in practice the residential bishop, to decide, in accordance with the instructions of the Holy See, under what circumstances and with what precautions attendance at non-Catholic schools may be tolerated.

It is certainly normal that the Holy See reserve to itself the supreme judgment in such an important matter of faith and morals. Positive directions in this, therefore, will be found in general documents for the whole Church, especially in encyclical letters, and also in particular documents sent to certain countries and dioceses.[19]

But since local conditions may reflect considerable divergencies, it is just as normal that the Holy See appoint the local ordinaries as the immediate judges in the practical applications of its own general directions in this matter.

The question whether these requirements apply to all kinds of schools, including universities, or only to elementary and intermediate schools, is still discussed by canonists. They also distinguish a double procedure for the exercise of this power by the ordinary. He can either pass judgment in each individual case, or simply lay down general rules applicable to the whole area of his jurisdiction.[20] For the particular scope of this study it will

[19] Cf. Pius XI, litt. encycl. *Divini illius magistri,* 31 dec. 1929—*AAS,* XXII (1930), 49-86; S.C. Ep. et Reg., instr. 21 iul. 1896—*Fontes,* n. 2031; S.C. de Prop. Fide, instr. (ad Vic. Ap. Societ. Mission. ad Exteros), a. 1659—*Fontes,* n. 4463; litt. encycl. (ad Ep. Hiberniae), 18 sept. 1819—*Fontes,* n. 4714; litt. (ad Archiep. Hiberniae), 16 ian. 1841—*Fontes,* n. 4787; litt. encycl. (ad Ep. Orient.), 20 mart. 1865—*Fontes,* n. 4863; instr. (ad Vic. Ap. Indiar. Orient.), 8 sept. 1869, n. 37—*Fontes,* n. 4876; litt. encycl. (ad Ep. Canad.), 14 mart. 1895—*Fontes,* n. 4932. Also *Acta et Decreta Concilii Plenarii Baltimorensis Tertii,* n. 198; *Acta et Decreta Concilii Provincialis Mechliniensis Quarti,* n. 223.

[20] Cf. Bouscaren-Ellis, *Canon Law* (Milwaukee: The Bruce Publishing Company, 1946), p. 705.

suffice to mention here and comment briefly, under what circumstances and with what precautions the instructions of the Holy See tolerate attendance at non-Catholic schools.

These circumstances are considered to exist when nearby there is no Catholic school suited to the real needs of the pupil who could not, without grave inconvenience, be sent elsewhere to receive his education as a Catholic. Moral theology teaches that the greater and more immediate the danger to faith and morals, the more compelling must be the circumstances to justify the attendance of Catholics at non-Catholic schools.

One can easily call to mind particular instances wherein the Church will allow Catholics to attend mixed or neutral schools, provided there is a sufficient reason and the danger of perversion is made remote. But what about attendance at an anti-Catholic or a non-Catholic denominational school?

No circumstances, not even the certainty of most serious damage, will ever justify attendance at an anti-Catholic institution, where the proximate danger to the faith can never be made remote for children or adolescents who are naturally unstable and easily impressionable.[21] For similar reasons attendance at a non-Catholic denominational school can not be tolerated unless the case be one of extreme necessity, such as when Catholics would be confronted with the alternative either of leaving the whole education to non-Catholics, or of being satisfied with a non-Catholic denominational school. It is evident that here especially efficient precautions will be required to make the proximate danger a remote one. If, however, notwithstanding all precautions, the danger of perversion remains proximate, then, no matter what sacrifices may be required, attendance at such schools would always appear to be forbidden. In such a case one would apply to these schools the natural law that radically prompts the unfavorable position towards anti-Catholic schools, and caused the Sacred Congregation for the Propagation of the Faith to issue the severe instruction about at

---

[21] Cf. *Acta et Decreta Concilii Provincialis Mechliniensis Quarti*, n. 223: ". . . numquam, nec ad gravissima damna vitanda, licitum est adire scholas perniciosas, in quibus videlicet periculum fidei et moribus ita immineat ut nullis cautelis removeri possit, . . ."

least one kind of denominational schools, the pagan ones, never to be tolerated.[22] An argument in support of the strict opinion in this matter may be found in the absolute tenor of canon 2319 in placing under a *latae sententiae* excommunication, reserved to the ordinary, all parents who knowingly present their children to be educated or trained in a non-Catholic religion.[23]

When the Church leaves room for the exceptional cases of Catholics attending non-Catholic schools it is not giving up any of its principles; it is merely tolerating a lesser evil, the non-Catholic school, in order to avoid a greater one, namely, that Catholics would be deprived of that secular knowledge which is necessary for their temporal welfare. If, however, one would try to make it appear that the insistence on Catholic schools for Catholic youth would always mean depriving them of a superior secular training, such as that which supposedly is given in non-Catholic schools, there seems at hand an answer with this double consideration. Suppose that Catholic schools really would provide a second-rate secular education, even then the Church would insist on the logic of Christian education. Taking into account man's final destiny, it would rather see its children less trained in temporal science than exposed to the loss of eternal happiness. But, in shifting from a theoretical concession to the reality of past and present history, one may present the challenge to anyone to point out the countries on the globe where the Catholic School System is in any way inferior to other institutions of learning.[24]

---

[22] C. P. pro Sin., 19 iul. 1838: "Omnino prohibeantur christiani adolescentes paganorum scholas frequentare, attento periculo perversionis et idolatriae."—*Fontes,* n. 4773. Similarly, in 1867, the same Sacred Congregation forbade Catholic youth to attend the schools of Oxford and Cambridge, since, at least at that time, the whole atmosphere of these institutions constituted a proximate danger to the faith and morals of Catholics. See Litt. encycl. ad Ep. Angliae, 6 aug. 1867—*Fontes,* n. 4868.

[23] "Subsunt excommunicationi latae sententiae Ordinario reservatae catholici . . . parentes vel parentum locum tenentes qui liberos in religione acatholica educandos vel instituendos scienter tradunt." The second paragraph of this canon moreover declares them suspect of heresy.

[24] Cf. S.C.S. Off., instr. (ad Ep. Stat. Foeder. Americae Septentrion.), 24 nov. 1875: "Est autem ad hoc omnium consensu nil tam necessarium, quam ut catholici ubique locorum proprias sibi scholas habeant, easque publicis scholis haud inferiores."—*Fontes,* n. 1046.

But, while by way of exception permitting Catholics to attend non-Catholic schools, the Holy See requires from both the parents and the local Church authorities definite precautions so as to make the inherent danger to faith and morals as remote as possible. Parents, the first responsible ones, must make constant inquiries concerning the teaching imparted to their children, by questioning them on the books used and the doctrines expounded in class; they shall likewise watch their children so as to shield them from any contacts with bad companions, and redouble their own educational efforts in the home. The bishops, on the other hand, shall see to it that Catholic pupils attending non-Catholic schools receive suitable religious instruction from a Catholic teacher after school hours, either in the classroom or in centers of catechetics.

In this connection one should insist upon the fact that, however general the Church's disapproval of neutral or mixed schools may be, it has never intended to blame the Catholic teachers in such schools. On the contrary, the Church is realistic enough to know that, as the result of certain circumstances, there will always be a number of its baptized children in civil public neutral or mixed schools. Even if the Catholic teachers in such schools may not be permitted to profess their own religious feelings, they will at least not harm the religious education elsewhere imparted to the Catholic pupils. Besides that, without any proselytizing on his part, the Catholic teacher in the civil public school will find in his professional and technical efficiency an excellent way to make himself a credit for his Church.[25]

Finally, it may be worthwhile to note that the general law of the Church does not invoke any penal sanctions against attendance at neutral or mixed schools. Of course, the Holy Office states that Catholic parents who neglect to give the necessary Christian training and education to their children, or who, without sufficient reason and without the necessary safeguards permit them to at-

---

[25] Cf. Joseph-Ernest Cardinal Van Roey, Archbishop of Malines: "Je vous salue et je vous bénis, instituteurs officiels qui êtes attachés à vos convictions religieuses et qui les faites passer dans votre mission d'éducateurs, conformément au voeu des parents qui vous confient leurs enfants."—*Au Service de l'Église. In den Dienst van de Kerk* (4 vols., Turnhout: N. V. Brepols, 1939-1940), III, p. 298.

tend non-Catholic schools, can not be absolved in the sacrament of penance.[26] But, as the Sacred Congregation itself explains it, this is but the expression of a traditional Catholic doctrine regarding penitents who lack the proper dispositions for absolution. Such parents must not be absolved as long as they are contumacious; but they should be absolved as soon as they have seriously promised amendment. Besides that, it is always within the power of the local ordinary to reserve for himself the absolution of this kind of sin, or to determine suitable penalties for parents who would be contumacious in this matter.[27] As for attendance at non-Catholic denominational schools, it suffice once again to refer to the above mentioned common law of the Church which states that Catholic parents who, knowing the law and its punishment, send their children to a school to be educated in a non-Catholic religion, incur *ipso facto* an excommunication the absolution from which is reserved to the ordinary.[28]

---

[26] S.C.S. Off., instr. (ad Ep. Stat. Foeder. Americae Septentrion.), 24 nov. 1875: "Hanc autem necessariam christianam institutionem et educationem liberis suis impertire quotquot parentes negligunt; aut qui frequentare eos sinunt tales scholas in quibus animarum ruina evitari non potest; aut tandem qui, licet schola catholica in eodem loco idonea adsit, apteque instructa, et parata, seu quamvis facultatem hebeant in alia regione prolem catholice educandi, nihilominus committunt eam scholis publicis, sine sufficienti causa, ac sine necessariis cautionibus, quibus periculum perversionis e proximo remotum fiat; eos, si contumaces fuerint, absolvi non posse in Sacramento Poenitentiae ex doctrina morali catholica manifestum est."—*Fontes,* n. 1046.

[27] *Canon 2221*: "Legislativam habentes potestatem, possunt intra limites suae iurisdictionis, non solum legem a se vel a decessoribus latam, sed etiam, ob peculiaria rerum adiuncta, legem tam divinam, quam ecclesiasticam a superiore potestate latam, in territorio vigentem, congrua poena munire aut poenam lege statutam aggravare."

[28] *Canon 2319,* § *1, 4°* : "Subsunt excommunicationi latae sententiae Ordinario reservatae catholici: . . . Parentes vel parentum locum tenentes qui liberos in religione acatholica educandos vel instituendos scienter tradunt." By reason of the second paragraph of this same canon such parents are also suspected of heresy and subject to the penalties of canon 2315, of which the principal consists in one's being barred from the exercise or performance of legally authorized ecclesiastical acts. Legally authorized ecclesiastical acts are the acts which by the law of the Church a member in good standing is authorized to exercise or perform.

PART TWO

Catholic Elementary Schools in Belgium

No part of the history of present-day Belgium can be fully understood without some preliminary acquaintance with the two thousand year old history of the people who now inhabit the kingdom of Belgium.[1]

Belgium as an entirely autonomous independent kingdom has existed only since 1830. Belgium as a country, and the Belgians as a people, existed long before. If human bones, fossils and tools can be accepted as conclusive proofs, the present-day territory of Belgium already had its inhabitants about 7000 B.C.

More is known about the Belgium of the pre-Christian era through Greek and Roman writers. Julius Caesar in his *De Bello Gallico* (57 B.C.) recorded that Gaul was divided into three parts, one of which was inhabited by the Belgians: *Gallia Belgica.* They resisted the attacks of the Roman legions for four years, and Caesar himself testified of them that they were "the bravest of all the people of Gaul."

With the so-called *Pax Romana* the Christian religion came to Belgium. It is known that at least one organized diocese, the See of Tongeren where the later Saint Materne was bishop, existed about the year 320.[2]

The fifth century brought with it the establishment of the house of Merovingian Kings. Following a period of feudalism, the High

---

[1] Cf. Horne-Keller, *History of the Belgian People* (New York: The International Historical Society, 1917); Van Bemmel, *Patria Belgica* (3 vols., Bruxelles: Bruylant-Christophe & Cie, 1873-1875); van der Essen, *Deux mille Ans d'Histoire* (Bruxelles: Éditions Universitaires, 1946); van der Essen, *A Short History of Belgium* (2. ed., Chicago: The University of Chicago Press, 1920).

[2] The present-day Belgian ecclesiastical province comprises the archdiocese of Malines which was erected in 1559, and the dioceses of Tournai (about 496), Liège (720) comprising the former diocese of Tongeren, and Bruges, Ghent, and Namur, all three erected in 1559.

Middle Ages saw the development of the independent communes. Little by little the barriers between them were broken down, and the way was prepared for union.

To find Belgium as a united political body one must wait until the fifteenth century when Philip the Good, the *Conditor Belgii,* succeeded in unifying all the Belgian provinces under one dynasty. It was under his reign and that of the other Dukes of Burgundy that Belgium developed into the most prosperous country in Europe, with Antwerp as "the greatest market of the North." Belgium at that time included the provinces of Belgium and Holland as we know them today, of Artois in France, the Grand Duchy of Luxemburg, the County of Burgundy, and all these provinces, such as Hainaut, which are now divided between France and Belgium.[8]

But, as a Flemish national song puts it, no thrones can stand forever. Deprived of a prosperity and culture never to be regained, the Belgians were subject to Spanish rule in the sixteenth and seventeenth centuries, to Austrian rule in the eighteenth century, to a French regime in 1792, and to a Dutch rule in 1815, before they were able to rebuild their national independence through the revolution of 1830.

Since the Constitution of the new Belgian State, and especially its stand towards religious and educational freedom, cannot be understood except as a violent reaction against the existing Dutch regime, it is necessary to examine briefly this Dutch-Belgian union.

---

[8] Today Belgium is divided into nine provinces. Four are Flemish: West-Flanders, East-Flanders, Antwerp, and Limburg. Four are Walloon: Hainaut, Namur, Liège, and Luxemburg. One, the province of Brabant, which includes the capital, Brussels, has a mixed population.

Covering an area of 11,775 square miles the Belgian population has increased from 3,785,000 in 1831 to 8,639,000 (U. N. estimate 1950), placing the density per square mile at 710, compared with 340 in Germany, and 270 in France.

Belgium's colony, the Belgian Congo, which is not an object of this study, has a population of 10,804,761 (in 1947) in an area of 904,757 square miles. With the Belgian Congo is now administratively united the United-Nations-trust territory of Ruanda-Urundi with 3,718,545 natives in an area of 19,536 square miles.

CHAPTER III

The Historical Background, the Dutch Rule 1815-1830

With the defeat of Napoleon at Waterloo in Belgium, on June 18, 1815, the curtain falls down on that intellectual, social, and political movement known as the French Revolution. The coalition of the European States prevailed over France and drove back her armies to their point of departure, Paris.

Since 1814, when the French troops evacuated Belgium, the Big Four of those days, England, Prussia, Austria, and Russia, agreed on certain basic principles. France was to be limited to the boundaries which she had held before her revolutionary conquests, and placed again under her former dynasty.

It had always been a principle of British policy that the territory at the mouths of the rivers Scheldt, Meuse, and Rhine, which empty into the North Sea opposite the mouth of the Thames, should never be under French or German control. Especially then, to prevent an eventual new expansion by France, these "Low Countries" were to be fortified as strongly as possible. According to the British view the best fortification could be the formation of a single buffer-state which would include both Belgian and Dutch territory. This solution would at the same time give England the long awaited opportunity to reward the Prince of Orange, Stadholder of Holland, who had lost his states of Nassau, and also to recompense the Dutch for certain lost colonies of theirs which England intended to keep under British rule.[1]

Without even consulting the Belgians in the matter, the Big Powers, on July 31, 1814, handed the Belgian provinces over to the Prince of Orange whom the Dutch had made their sovereign the year before. The Congress of Vienna (1815), losing complete sight of the Belgians' long struggle for unification and sense of in-

---

[1] Cf. Steinmetz, *Englands Anteil an der Trennung der Niederlände* (Den Haag: M. Nijhoff, 1930).

dependence, sanctioned the existence of this United Kingdom of the Netherlands, and recognized the sovereignty of the Prince of Orange under the title of King William I (1772-1843). To guarantee the success of this diplomatic "European solution" the Allies made William pledge himself to grant Belgium political liberty, respect for her traditional religion, and complete equality within the union.

From the political viewpoint, the setting up of the new state was a grand idea. Nothing could do more to maintain peace in the Europe of 1815 than such a neutral buffer-state. For the interested peoples themselves it almost looked like a new edition of the old states of Burgundy that had brought them such prosperity. In the economical field, too, the new kingdom could look forward to the brightest future. The well developed agricultural system and the mineral wealth of the Belgians, together with the commercial skill of the Dutch, would most logically lead to the height of economical and material success.[2]

But, this Belgian-Dutch union was to show, in a way unparalleled in European history, that material elements alone are not sufficient for building and keeping a nation strong and united. The "complete and intimate fusion," of which Metternich (1773-1859) and his fellow-diplomats had dreamed, could never succeed, because moral factors were keeping the two peoples apart. Since the time of their separation in the sixteenth century, the Dutch in the North and the Belgians in the South had been developing along diverging lines. Differing in language, religion, temperament, and political habits, the two groups did not want to be united. The utopian character of that "arrangement for a European object" was clearly understood by some diplomats as by the one who already in 1815 wrote to his government: "This marriage of convenience took place without any love on either side, and it is very doubtful if it will ever make even one of the parties happy."[3]

---

[2] Cf. Colenbrander, *De Afscheiding van Belgie* (Amsterdam: J. M. Meulenhoff, 1936); Demoulin, *Guillaume Ier et la Transformation économique des Provinces belges, 1815-1830* (Liège: Bibliothèque de l'Université, 1938).

[3] Marquis de la Tour du Pin, French ambassador at Brussels, in his report of Sept. 22, 1815: "Ce marriage de convenance s'est fait sans aucun amour

A more far-seeing government could perhaps have brought about at least a collaboration between the two parts of the new state. However, William I, in spite of his qualities as an organizer, failed because in his authoritarian mind "union" was in reality nothing but placing the Belgian provinces under the dominion of the North, less extensive in territory and more sparsely populated.

The trouble started immediately when William wanted to extend the Dutch constitutional regime to the Belgians. The Dutch Fundamental Law of March 30, 1814, was of such an autocratic character that the chances of its being accepted in Belgium were very small. The Powers therefore imposed on William the obligation of adapting this constitution to the needs created by the territorial extension of his country. The sincere efforts of the King in this might have been crowned with success, if it had not been for the religious issues involved.

The draft-proposal of the adapted constitution provided freedom and equality for all creeds. Immediately the Belgian clergy, led by the Bishop of Ghent, Maurice de Broglie (1766-1821), unleashed a violent campaign against these new constitutional stipulations.[4] Under this influence the "Assembly of prominent Citizens," consulted by the King, refused to legalize this religious

---

de part et d'autre, et il est douteux s'il fera le bonheur d'aucune des deux parties."—Quoted by Van Kalken, *Histoire du Royaume des Pays-Bas et de la Révolution belge de 1830* (Bruxelles: J. Lebègue et Cie, 1910), p. 30. See also van der Essen, *La Belgique dans le Royaume des Pays-Bas, 1814-1830* (Bruxelles: La Lecture au Foyer, 1924).

[4] The attitude of the Belgian Hierarchy in its opposition to this constitutional equality for all creeds cannot be just explained by calling them "men of the Old Regime." Cf. Schmitz, *Guillaume Ier et la Belgique* (Bruxelles: Ad. Goemaere, 1945), p. 211. No doubt, as Belgian citizens the bishops also opposed "civil" equality for all creeds, since this would open the completely Catholic Belgian provinces to Protestant civil administrators from the North. But we deem it unjust to overlook the deeper motive of the resistance of the Catholic clergy to a constitution based upon that religious indifferentism, which proclaims not just the civil but also the "dogmatical" equality of all creeds.—Cf. Terlinden, *Guillaume Ier. Roi des Pays-Bas, et l'Eglise Catholique en Belgique, 1814-1830* (2 vols., Bruxelles: A. Dewit, 1906), II, pp. 221-222, note; I, pp. 87-89, 103-105.

equality, and rejected the new constitution by a large majority on August 18, 1815. But, on August 24, William declared that the Act was passed.[5]

But, this official promulgation of the new Fundamental Law did not end the opposition of the Catholic hierarchy. Immediately the bishops published a "Doctrinal Decision," forbidding Catholics to take the oath of fidelity to this Constitution. One of the main reasons for their protest was art. 226, stating that "public instruction is the constant care of the government." The episcopal document stated: "To swear to observe and maintain a law which gives a non-Catholic sovereign the right to regulate public instruction is tantamount to handing over to him complete control of education, and shamefully betraying the most cherished interests of the Catholic Church."[6] Later experience was to prove how justified was the stand of the Hierarchy on this point.

After vainly trying to gain the support of the Holy See in his struggle with the Belgian episcopacy, the King started to persecute the clergy, going even so far as to order the Bishop of Ghent to be deported for contumacy (1817). Only in 1821 some kind of agreement was reached when the government conceded what Archbishop de Méan had been asking for since the beginning, namely that the oath of fidelity to the Constitution should be binding only

---

[5] Among the 1,603 delegates 280 abstained. Of the 1,323 voters, 796 voted against and only 527 were in favor of the views of the King. Among the 796 negative voters 126 gave as their main motive for their negative vote their opposition to religious equality. The frustrated King then ordered that all who had abstained from voting should be counted as voting for the act; the 126 "religious" voters should not count, as the principle of religious liberty had been imposed by the Congress of Vienna, and had to be observed by all. Thanks to this system of counting the votes, later on in history ironically called "Dutch arithmetic," William obtained 807 votes in favor and only 670 against.—Cf. Van Kalken, *op. cit.*, p. 47.

[6] "Jurer d'observer et de maintenir une loi qui attribue au souverain, et à un souverain que ne professe pas notre sainte religion, le droit de régler l'instruction publique, . . . c'est lui livrer à discrétion l'enseignement public dans toutes ses branches, c'est trahir honteusement les plus chers intérêts de l'Église catholique."—Quoted in de Gerlache, *Histoire du Royaume des Pays-Bas depuis 1814 jusqu'en 1830* (3 vols., Bruxelles: M. Hayez, 2. ed., 1842), I, p. 318.

from the civil point of view, leaving the dogmatical judgment on the matter untouched.

If there had been any real desire on the part of King William to respect the conscience of the Belgian Catholics and to bring about a sincere collaboration between the two peoples, he would have inaugurated a policy aimed at eliminating the religious differences. On the contrary, under the inspiration of his biased counselors he continued his policy of oppression, excelling especially in the suppression of educational liberty.

No kind of education was to escape the King's fanatical urge to set up a state monopoly. He did not exempt even the training of the Catholic clergy, which, by the general canons of the Church, specifically expressed by the Council of Trent, belonged exclusively to the ecclesiastical authorities. By means of a series of "royal decrees" minor seminaries were suppressed and a State institution was erected under the name of "Philosophical College" in which every aspirant for the priesthood was forced to take a course of two years before he could be admitted to a major seminary. Other decrees brought higher and intermediate education also under the total control of the State.[7]

For the particular scope of this study, however, special attention must be given to the King's system of monopolizing the primary education. In this matter it was the whole Dutch policy to implant into the Belgian public life the Dutch law of April 3, 1806, which sanctioned the monopoly of the State. Small concessions to local needs or brutal measures like the suppression of religious teaching congregations, were but tactical moves in the steady progress towards the ideal of complete State control.[8]

Anyone familiar with the traditional freedom-loving and Catholic character of the Belgian public life would have doubted from the very beginning the success of such an enterprise. But to fully understand the later reaction of the Belgian Constitution against

---

[7] Cf. de Gerlache, *op. cit.*, I, pp. 371-373. Compare with Schroeder, *Canons and Decrees of the Council of Trent* (St. Louis: B. Herder & Co., 1941), p. 175.

[8] Cf. Stokman, *De Religieuzen en de Onderwijspolitiek der Regeering in het Vereenigd Koninkrijk der Nederlanden* (1814-1830) ('s Gravenhage: Het R. K. Centraal Bureau voor Onderwijs en Opvoeding, 1935), particularly pp. 29-46, 141; de Gerlache, *op. cit.*, I, pp. 368, 377.

this State monopoly, it is necessary to review here briefly the Dutch elementary school system as contained in the legislation of 1806.[9]

The Dutch school legislation of 1806 contained, in addition to the general provisions of the law itself, other general administrative regulations of which the first one was the basic and the most important.

A. THE SCHOOL INSPECTION LAW

The law of April 3, 1806, composed of only 21 articles, was entirely dedicated to the organization of the inspection of schools. The whole of the primary instruction was in the hands of a hierarchy of inspectors, from the inspector-general through provincial committees of inspectors down to the last district-inspector. All were salaried and responsible functionaries of the State: the district-inspector reported to the provincial committee which in turn was responsible to the inspector-general and the minister of education, appointed by the King.

1. The District-Inspector

The district-inspector was in charge of the entire primary education in his little district. He had to make at least two personal visits to each school every year. Besides that, he had absolute control over the appointment of teachers who had to subject themselves not only to a general examination for admission to the teaching profession but also to a second "special examination."

The license for general admission, the so-called "license of capability," was granted to a person of good moral standards after an examination before the provincial committee composed exclusively of the various district-inspectors. Without this general license nobody could even apply for any teaching position. And only these State-inspectors were entitled to issue such license.

---

[9] Reference for this is made to Ducpétiaux, *De l'état de l'Instruction primaire et populaire en Belgique, comparé avec celui de l'Instruction en Allemagne, en Prusse, en Suisse, en France, en Hollande et aux États-Unis* (Bruxelles: Meline, Caus et Cie, 1838), II, pp. 274-301 (hereafter cited *De l'état de l'Instruction*).—Cf. also Stokman, *op. cit.*, pp. 29-34.

This "general license of capability" made one a candidate-teacher. If the candidate wanted to teach in what the law called a "private school," he needed an "authorization" by the local civil authority which in turn could grant this solely to persons recommended by the district-inspector.[10] The candidate applying for a teaching position in a public school was to receive his "nomination" after another special examination before a jury of which the district-inspector was always the most influential member. In cases wherein he disagreed with the views of the other jury-members he could appeal to the minister of education.

Once authorized or nominated, both private and public school teachers had to appear in person before the district-inspector alone, to have their "special admission," in the words of the law, justified.

After he had taken up a position, no teacher, either public or private, could qualify for any kind of promotion, without recourse again to the district-inspector, who was either the president or the influential member of all the committees involved.

Finally, also the revocation or the suspension of a teacher was pronounced by the local or provincial authorities, . . . in accordance with the recommendations of the district-inspector.

2. The Provincial Committee of Inspectors

Three times a year all the district-inspectors of the province met in the provincial capital under the presidency of the governor of the province. Each inspector presented a report on conditions in his district and proposed to the assembly whatever practical decisions might be needed. The committee then investigated if the acts of each inspector were performed in accordance with the provincial regulations, and also drew up rules for a uniform application of these regulations. After straightening out the administrative matters under its jurisdiction, the committee finally made up its annual report to be sent, with the necessary suggestions, to the central government.

---

[10] Under this Dutch system the only difference between public and private schools was that the latter received no financial aid from civil authorities. But as far as State-control was concerned, all schools were treated as public.

3. The Central Government

The Inspector-General for Primary Instruction acted for the Minister of Education who was appointed by the King. If necessary, the central government convened a "General Assembly for Primary Instruction," to which each provincial committee was to send a delegate. All inspectors were appointed by this Minister of Education.

B. THE GENERAL SCHOOL REGULATIONS

The school law found its complement in the general regulations issued by the central government as the necessary pattern for all provincial and local school regulations.[11] The particular points of interest for this study are the following: This general regulation first of all established the so-called "local committees of supervision"; it reserved further to the central government the right to authorize the books to be used in all public schools; and finally excluded all religious training from any public school.

1. The Local Committees of Supervision

Each district-inspector was given the right to establish "local committees of supervision" in all places with several public and private schools (art. 10). Such committees were authorized to lay down a "special regulation," which simply took the form of an adaptation of the general and provincial regulations to the particular circumstances and needs of the local schools (art. 21). But in order to prevent any diminution of the authority of the district-inspector the same article specified that these special regulations were to be sent to the provincial committees which in turn were to forward them, with the necessary amendments, to the Minister of Education.

---

[11] Four in number they were known as Regulations A, B, C, and D. The regulations B, C, and D were only clarifications of the general rules of Regulation A which was entitled "Regulation for all that concerns primary instruction and its allied institutions in the entire Dutch republic."

2. The Authorization of School Books

Only the central government could authorize the books. to be used in public schools, and even the ones to be used in private schools. From the authorized list of books, published by the government, the provincial committee chose those that were to be used exclusively in all public schools of the province. The teacher in the private schools could make his own choice of books, provided he notified the district-inspector. This inspector in turn had these books checked by the provincial committee or, if necessary, even by the central governmental authority (art. 24).

3. The Mixed School

All positive religious instruction was excluded from the public schools (art. 21 and 23). Of course art. 22 accepted the principle, common in those days, that all elementary education should have as its final aim the moral and religious formation of youth, "the practice of all social and Christian virtues." All other European countries in the early 19th century, Protestants as well as Catholics, believed in the need for religious denominational schools to attain that Christian education. Even when there were children of different religious beliefs in attendance, the link between church and school was never broken. The regular teacher gave the religious instruction in accordance with his own creed and that of the majority of the pupils, while religious instruction of the other pupils was provided by their own religious minister at fixed hours reserved for him in their respective class-rooms in the school building. Holland, on the contrary, proclaimed the principle of the mixed school where only "common moral principles" were to be taught while at the same time children were to be given an opportunity to receive outside the school the proper dogmatical teaching of their particular denomination.

That such a school system would never be accepted by the Belgians should have been clear to everyone who knew their political and religious traditions.[12]

---

[12] The adaptations of this law to particular circumstances in Belgium were only concessions of a minor nature. Cf. Bosch, *Essai sur la Liberté de l'Enseignement et sur les Principes Généraux d'une Loi Organique de*

A law that justly could be called "the law of the governmental inspector-dictator" was not only repugnant to everyone believing in the educational rights of the individual and the family, but it also was openly and flagrantly opposed to the tradition of a people whose periods of national prosperity had always been connected with wide local autonomy. The veneer of authority of the so-called local committees of supervision was in practice not even a small concession to parental or local supervision in a school system of perfect State monopoly.

Besides that, to propose the mixed school as the ideal for a totally Catholic population was not only contrary to the traditional philosophy of Christian education, but also reflected a political blunder such as could be made only by the successor of the despotic Joseph II and the caesaropapist Bonaparte.

A failure to appreciate the principles of human psychology, coupled with religious fanaticism, prevented an outstanding organizer from becoming a great King. Leading the people in their resistance to King William, the Belgian bishops were marching along the lines of the best Catholic and Belgian tradition.[13] And it was this Dutch policy in religious and educational matters that contributed, as much as any other grievance, to change the passive resistance of the Belgians into the popular insurrection of 1830.

---

l'Instruction Publique, précédé d'un Coup d'oeil sur la Situation actuelle du Royaume des Pays-Bas (Bruxelles, 1829); Sluys, *Geschiedenis van het Onderwijs in de drie Graden in Belgie tijdens de Fransche Overheersching en de Regeering van Willem I* (Gent: Koninklijke Vlaamsche Academie voor Taal en Letterkunde, 1912); Stokman, *De Religieuzen en de Onderwijspolitiek der Regeering in het Vereenigd Koninkrijk der Nederlanden* (1814-1830), pp. 271-292, 310.

[13] The writer here subscribes to the traditional opinion of the historians in their judgment on this particular period of Belgian history. His adherence to their severe sentence concerning the religious and educational policy of King William was even confirmed by a reading of Schmitz, *Guillaume Ier et la Belgique* (Bruxelles: Ad. Goemaere, 1945) who tried to correct what he called the partiality of practically all authors on this subject. The writer found less "partiality" and "besmirching" in the masterwork on the subject, Terlinden, *Guillaume Ier, Roi des Pays-Bas, et l'Église catholique en Belgique* (*1814-1830*) (Bruxelles: A. Dewit, 1906) than in the explanation Schmitz gives for the conduct of the Belgian hierarchy, which to him was but the expression of a reactionary and old-regime spirit (p. 211).

CHAPTER IV

The Belgian Constitution (1831) and Freedom of Instruction

When the negotiations between the Holy See and the Dutch King finally resulted in a concordat on June 18, 1827, it was too late to hope for any true reconciliation between William and his Catholic subjects. The break between them, brought about officially by the protest of the hierarchy against the school-decrees of 1825, could never be mended. William's unfair application of the concordat increased the discontent of the Catholics.

But, strong as this Catholic opposition was, it would never of itself have resulted in a violent revolution. The way was finally paved for this when the government in the year 1827 injured also the interests of the Liberal minority which at first had applauded and even encouraged the King in his persecution of the Church. Although most Belgian Liberals professed the Catholic religion in their private life, their anticlericalism, based upon the rationalistic philosophy of the eighteenth century, aimed at the elimination of any Church-influence in the public life of the nation and made them the protagonists of the official neutral and mixed school. But the time came when the government saw its former Liberal supporters changed into its most violent opponents. Apart from the oppression of the Church and its schools, which in no way affected them, there were the following grievances which the Liberals felt keenly.

Although twice as numerous the Belgians were allowed only the same number of deputies in the country's States-General as the Dutch. Knowledge of the Dutch language was at once made obligatory for all public officials. The majority of the governmental institutions were located in Holland and practically all positions in them were reserved solely for the Dutch. The burden of the public debt of the old Dutch provinces was meanwhile partly transferred to the Belgian provinces, and brought about a system of taxation that was far too onerous for the southern provinces.

But, what finally made the Liberals see the autocratic nature of the Dutch policy was the fact that the government stifled any criticism by placing the press under the arbitrary control of governmental courts. This "nationalized" press, attacking as it did every Belgian who had the misfortune to disagree with the government, could no longer be accepted by men who proclaimed themselves champions of the individualistic "Declaration of the Rights of Man and of Citizens" of 1789. From the prison of the Petits-Carmes in which he was confined for violations of the Dutch press-laws, the anticlerical Liberal leader, Louis de Potter (1792-1869), advocated the union of Catholics and Liberals against the common enemy. The writing was on the wall for the Dutch rule in Belgium when in 1828 Catholics and Liberals, forgetting their differences, joined forces. The "Union of the Opposition" was born.[1]

This fusion of opposing interests was more readily accomplished because most Catholics, under the influence of Lamennais' (1782-1854) teachings, but especially under the pressure of the circumstances, had totally abandoned their stand of 1815 and had rallied to the principle of "liberty in all and for all." In 1815 Catholics condemned the so-called religious freedom as opening the way to dogmatical indifferentism. Now the events of the last ten years were pressing them to fight for that same freedom as a way to safeguard the existence of their Church.

The ecclesiastical authorities opposed this Union of the Opposition that once was described as a "monstrous alliance between contemporary and gothic ideas, between freedom and absolutism, between life and death."[2] Distrusting the Liberals who proclaimed themselves the upholders of the revolutionary principles of 1789, both the Holy See and the Belgian hierarchy feared that soon

---

[1] Cf. de Potter, *Révolution belge de 1828 à 1839* (3 vols., Bruxelles: Cans & Cie, 1839); de Potter, *Union des Catholiques et des Libéraux* (Bruxelles: Cans & Cie, 1829); du Bus de Warnaffe, *Au Temps de l'Unionisme* (Tournai: Casterman, 1944); Harsin, *Essai sur l'Opinion publique en Belgique de 1815 à 1830* (Charleroi: La Terre Wallonne, 1930).

[2] Quoted by Van Kalken, *Histoire du Royaume des Pays-Bas et de la Révolution belge de 1830,* p. 90.

lawful and peaceful protest would take on a revolutionary character. Right now in 1828 the Catholics, reminded by their bishops of the traditional Catholic teaching concerning civic duties towards any public authority, wished to employ lawful means only and therefore suggested the drawing up and presentation of petitions from all classes of society. Hundreds of petitions, bearing more than 40,000 signatures, poured into the offices of the States-General, demanding liberty of education, freedom of the press, freedom of association and peaceable assembly, and the correction of other abuses. While these petitions were being circulated the law-abiding Catholics were able to maintain perfect order in the country. But, it was precisely this state of affairs which deceived the King. On a tour which he made through the Belgian provinces to gather first-hand information about the state of the public opinion, he was received with such respect that he convinced himself that the petitioning was not a spontaneous movement. He went even so far as to declare at Liège on June 23, 1829, that the conduct of the petitioners was infamous.[3]

William here lost his last opportunity of setting the public mind at rest. Concessions from him, which indeed could have solved the whole problem in 1828, came too late in 1829. When it became evident that no serious reforms could be expected from the King, the resistance of the Belgians turned into a truly national movement the direction of which passed from the hands of the peaceful Catholic majority into those of the revolutionary Liberal minority.

The conciliatory attitude of the Catholic hierarchy was powerless to control the popular movement. What is more, the local clergy not only allowed themselves to be swept along in this new revolutionary current, but were the prime movers in organizing further petitions subscribed this time by more than 300,000 impatient Belgians.[4]

---

[3] Cf. Van Kalken, *op. cit.*, p. 97.

[4] Cf. de Gerlache, *Histoire du Royaume des Pays-Bas,* II, pp. 6-13; de Nothomb, *Essai historique et politique sur la Révolution belge* (2 vols., Bruxelles-Leipzig: C. Muquardt, 1876); Rodenbach, *Épisodes de la Révolution dans les Flandres, 1829, 1830, 1831* (Bruxelles: L. Hauman & Cie, 1833); Van Kalken, *Histoire de Belgique des Origines à 1914* (Bruxelles: Office de Publicité, 1944), p. 487; Van Langenhove, *La Volonté nationale belge en 1830* (Paris-Bruxelles: G. van Oest & Cie, 1917).

The "Royal Message" of December 11, 1829, brought William's answer: a categorical "No." Similarly, only a few days before, when one of the most loyal and outstanding Belgian citizens tried to wring some last-minute concessions from the King, he had been rebuffed with this answer: "I am King of the Low Countries; I know my rights; I know my duties; and by all means I will uphold this constitution that I have sworn to defend."[5] The moral break between the Dutch King and his Belgian subjects was complete, and the smallest opportunity would suffice to change it into a total political disunion.

In 1830 the French Revolution of the "Three Glorious Days" (July 27-29) overthrew the dynasty of the Bourbons reëstablished by the Allies. Up to that day the Belgian "Union of Opposition" had always confined itself to peaceful protest. But now, spurred on by this French example, a chain of popular reactions was set in motion and nobody could stop it. On August 25 of the same year a riot broke out in Brussels and brought on the revolution which culminated in the conflicts between the Dutch troops and the people of Brussels assisted by reënforcement of volunteers from the provinces. The whole country rose up. Within two months the Dutch troops were driven out of the southern provinces and the Belgians were free.[6]

From September 24, 1830, an administrative committee took over the rule of the Belgian provinces. On September 26 this committee became the Provisional Government, and independent Belgium existed *de facto*. The formal proclamation of this independence took place on October 4, when the Provisional Government declared that "the Belgian provinces, forcibly detached from Holland, now form an independent State; that the central committee will as soon as possible prepare a draft-constitution; and

---

[5] "Je suis roi des Pays-Bas; je connais mon droit; je connais mon devoir; et je maintiendrai, de tous mes moyens, cette constitution que j'ai jurée."—de Gerlache, *op. cit.*, II, p. 20.

[6] Cf. de Gerlache, *op. cit.*, II, pp. 35-81; Demoulin, *Les Journées de septembre 1830 à Bruxelles et en Province* (Liège: Bibliothèque de l'Université, 1934); Willequet, *1830, Naissance de l'État belge* (Bruxelles: Éditions du Temple, 1950).

that a National Congress will immediately be convened."[7] On October 12, all restrictive measures concerning the freedom of instruction were abolished by the Provisional Government. Four days later a complete freedom of association and of peaceable assembly, of religion, of instruction, and of the press was proclaimed.[8]

On November 10, 1830, the National Congress, composed of 200 members directly elected by about 30,000 voters, assembled in the hall of the former States-General in Brussels to take over the legislative power from the Provisional Government. For three months this National Congress worked at drawing up a Constitution which was finally promulgated on February 7, 1831.[9] The true spirit of conciliation between Catholics and Liberals became evident when the new Constitution proclaimed the absolute freedom of worship (art. 14, 15, 16, 117), and of the press (art. 18), which the Liberals put first, and also freedom of education (art. 17), and of peaceable assembly and association (art. 19 and 20), which were two things especially dear to the Catholics.

---

[7] "... que les provinces de la Belgique, violemment détachées de la Hollande, constituent un état indépendant; que le comité central s'occupera au plus tôt d'un projet de constitution, et qu'un congrès national sera immédiatement convoqué."—de Gerlache, *op. cit.*, II, p. 84.

[8] Cf. de Gerlache, *op. cit.*, II, p. 85. Compare with van Hogendorp, *De Ontwikkeling, 13 December 1830-26 Januari 1831* ('s Gravenhage: W. K. Mandemaker, 1830-1831).

[9] Practically all historians, non-Catholics as well as Catholics, subscribe to the opinion that the greater part of this National Congress, 140 out of 200, was made up of Catholics. These Catholics, with 13 priests among them, were advocates of "liberty in all and for all" in conformity with the teachings of Lamennais. Among the Liberal minority one can distinguish two groups: the stronger professed the same ideas of liberty as the Catholics; the other was made up of a small number of fanatics whose fondest dream was that of subjecting the Catholic Church to the civil power. But, in those days it would be wrong to stress political opinions. The defense of the independence and the liberty won by the revolution was more important than the insistence on party names. Cf. de Lichtervelde, *Le Congrès National, l'Oeuvre et les Hommes* (Bruxelles: Renaissance du Livre, 1945); du Bus de Warnaffe, *Physionomie du Congrès National* (Bruxelles: A. Dewit, 1930); du Bus de Warnaffe, *Le Congrès National* (Bruxelles: Librairie nationale d'Art et d'Histoire, 1931).

The importance of this Belgian Constitution can not be overestimated. A study of contemporary international history shows that this basic law, second only in antiquity to that of the United States of America, and the oldest now in force in Europe, has enjoyed in its long history an exceptional measure of success.[10] The Belgian national historian, Henri Pirenne (1862-1935), could truthfully write without being accused of any nationalistic chauvinism: "It is the most complete and purest type of a parliamentary and liberal constitution. During half a century it has been a model of its kind, a masterpiece of political wisdom. The states which, in the course of the nineteenth century, have revised or elaborated their institutions along parliamentary lines have been directly and often profoundly influenced by it. Not one of them, however, has stretched so far the consequences of these principles; not one has granted such a large measure of freedom, nor given over so completely the government of the nation to the nation itself."[11] This basic law, adopted 120 years ago, still continues to be, with some amendments, the first law of the country, and this fact alone proves its importance from the national viewpoint.

In seven titles the Constitution treats successively of the territory and its subdivisions; the Belgians and their rights; the legislative, executive and judicial powers; the finances; the armed forces; some general provisions; and the revision of the Consti-

---

[10] For a comparison between the Constitution of the U. S. A. and the Belgian Fundamental Law, see Reed, *Government and Politics of Belgium* (Yonkers-on-Hudson, N. Y.: World Book Company, 1924), pp. 24-26. Cf. also Reed, Introduction to de Lichtervelde, *Léopold First, the Founder of Modern Belgium* (New York-London: The Century Company, 1930), pp. VII-X.

[11] ". . . la constitution belge apparait comme le type le plus complet et le plus pur que l'on puisse imaginer d'une constitution parlementaire et libérale. Durant un demi-siècle elle a passé en son genre pour un chef-d'oeuvre de sagesse politique. Elle a exercé une action directe et souvent profonde sur tous les États qui, au cours du XIXe siècle, ont remanié ou élaboré leurs institutions suivant les principes du parlementarisme. Aucun d'eux pourtant n'a poussé aussi loin qu'elle les conséquences de ces principes, dispensé aussi largement la liberté, et abandonné aussi entièrement le gouvernement de la nation à la nation elle-même."—*Histoire de Belgique* (7 vols., Bruxelles: Lamertin, 1909-1932), VI, p. 442.

tution. Of particular importance are articles 4 to 24 of Title II concerning the Belgian citizens and their rights, especially the ones dealing in detail with religion and education. Individual physical liberty, inviolability of domicile, respect for private property, freedom of religion, freedom of speech, freedom of education, freedom of the press, the right of peaceable assembly, association, and petition, the inviolability of the mails, the freedom of using any of the languages current in Belgium, were all guaranteed. No conditions were attached to the granting of these freedoms, in order to give the citizens unlimited liberty in their initiative. It was only when they abused these freedoms that the citizens were liable to punishment.

The articles which determine the relations between the Catholic Church and the new State are: Art. 14 guaranteeing religious freedom and freedom of speech; art. 15 excluding all compulsory observance of religion; art. 16 assuring the Church's freedom from State interference with clerical appointments, but insisting on the temporal precedence of the civil marriage ceremony. These basic articles find their complement in art. 117 concerning payment by the State of salaries and pensions of the clergy of the recognized Catholic, Protestant, and Jewish religions.[12]

---

[12] *Art. 14.* Religious liberty and the freedom of public worship, as well as free expression of opinion in all matters, are guaranteed, unless crimes are committed in the use of these liberties.

Art. 15. No one shall be compelled to join in any manner whatever in the forms or ceremonies of any religion, nor to observe its days of rest.

Art. 16. The State shall not interfere either in the appointment or in the installation of the ministers of any religion whatever, nor shall it forbid them to correspond with their superiors or publish their proceedings, subject to the ordinary responsibility of the press and of publication.—Civil marriage shall always precede the religious ceremony, except in cases to be established by law if found necessary.

Art. 117. The salaries and pensions of the ministers of religion shall be paid by the State; the sums necessary to meet this expenditure shall be entered annually in the budget.

The translation of these articles is taken from Vincent, *Constitution of the Kingdom of Belgium,* translated and supplied with an introduction and notes.—Supplement to the *Annals of the American Academy of Political and Social Science,* VII (1896), n. 3 (Philadelphia: American Academy of Political and Social Science, 1896).

These articles make it clear that in Belgium there is neither complete separation nor complete union between Church and State, although each remains independent in its own sphere. The Belgian regime is rather composed of elements taken from both these extreme solutions.[13]

Did such a liberal constitution of a Catholic country come under the condemnations of Liberalism issued by the Holy See?[14] All confusion about this matter finally disappeared when, in 1879, Pope Leo XIII, former papal nuncio at Brussels, declared to the Belgian government: "The works of men are by no means perfect; evil and good exist side by side, just as error and truth. Thus it is with the Belgian Constitution. It upholds some principles which no pope could approve of; but the state of Catholicity in Belgium, after an experience of half a century, proves that in the modern society the system of liberty in that country is the best suited to the needs of the Church. The Belgian Catholics must therefore not only refrain from attacking the Constitution, but should uphold it."[15]

---

[13] Cf. Claeys Boúúaert-Simenon, *Manuale Juris Canonici* (3 vols., 4. ed., Gandae et Leodii: apud auctores in seminariis Gandavensi et Leodiensi, 1934), I, p. 66; Thonissen, *La Constitution belge annotée* (3. ed., Bruxelles: Christophe-Bruylant, 1879); Van Hove, *Les Fabriques d'Église et le Temporel du Culte catholique en Belgique* (lithographed: T. I, Louvain, 1908-1911); van Mol, *Manuel de Droit constitutionnel de la Belgique* (12. ed., Liège: G. Thone, 1949); Van Overloop, *Exposé des Motifs de la Constitution belge* (Bruxelles: A. Goemaere, 1864).

[14] Gregorius XVI, litt. encycl. *Mirari vos,* 15 aug. 1832, referring to Liberalism as to a "pestilentissimus error"—Denzinger-Bannwart, *Enchiridion,* n. 1614; Pius IX, *Syllabus seu Collectio errorum modernorum,* prop. 55: "Ecclesia a statu statusque ab Ecclesia seiungendus est."—Denzinger-Bannwart, *Enchiridion,* n. 1755. Cf. Schmidlin, *Papstgeschichte der neuesten Zeit, t. 2. Papsttum und Päpste gegenüber den modernen Strömungen. Pius IX und Leo XIII, 1846-1903* (München, 1934).

[15] Cf. Balau, *Soixante-dix Ans d'Histoire contemporaine de Belgique, 1815-1884* (4. ed., Louvain, 1890), p. 310.

This clear statement of the Pope did not succeed in preventing the Liberals from upholding their old opinion that the Belgian Constitution was certainly condemned by the Holy See. Cf. de Laveleye in the introductory remarks to Juste, *Le Congrès de Belgique, 1830-1831* (2 vols., Bruxelles: Librairie européenne C. Muquardt, 1880), I, pp. c-d, who wrote about the Catholics

This had been the stand, from the very beginning, of the Belgian hierarchy in general and especially of the future Cardinal Engelbert Sterckx (1792-1867) who in 1832 became the Archbishop of Malines. In his opinion Pope Gregory XVI had condemned only the "total" separation between Church and State and that "dogmatical" freedom of religion which proclaims all religions of equal theological value. But, Sterckx explained, there was no such complete separation between Church and State in Belgium, and art. 14 of the Constitution was not meant to be a philosophical principle but only a measure to regulate practical conduct among citizens. Art. 5, "All powers emanate from the people," was to be understood in the sense that all rulers received their authority from God, but through the intervention of the people. Even the absolute temporal precedence of the civil marriage ceremony was condoned by Sterckx as an inevitable temporary concession in view of the need for social security in the Belgium of 1831, for the text of the Constitution itself made provision for a law to safeguard the freedom of the churches in exceptional cases, such as that of a marriage at the point of death. Similar interpretations of all other constitutional rules made the then vicar-general Sterckx write in 1831: "No article of the Constitution is contrary to the Catholic principles and the interests of the Church."[16]

The only constitutional law concerning education is contained

---

of 1831: ". . . à cette époque d'énivrement, ils oublièrent leurs dogmes, leurs traditions, leur histoire. Grégoire XVI le leur rappela durement dans la mémorable Encyclique de 1832, expression exacte de la doctrine des Péres et des Conciles."

[16] "Aucun article de la Constitution n'est contraire aux principes catholiques et aux intérêts de l'Église."—Cited by Simon, *Le Cardinal Sterckx et son Temps (1792-1867)* (2 vols., Wetteren: Editions Scaldis, 1950), I, p. 166; see also pp. 228-254. Cf. De Buck, *Les Principes catholiques et la Constitution belge* (Bruxelles: Vromant, 1878); de Moreau, *L'Église en Belgique des Origines au Début du XXe Siècle* (Bruxelles: Édition universelle, 1944), p. 226; *La Séparation de l'Église et de l'État en France. Exposé et Documents. Livre blanc du Saint-Siège* (Rome, 1905); Simon, *L'Église catholique et les Débuts de la Belgique indépendante* (Wetteren: Éditions Scaldis, 1949); Sterckx, Card., *La Constitution belge et l'Encyclique de Grégoire XVI. Deux Lettres sur nos Libertés constitutionelles,* Malines, 1864.

in art. 17: "There shall be freedom of opinion in teaching; all measures preventing this are forbidden; the repression of offenses shall be regulated only by law. Public instruction given at the expense of the State shall likewise be regulated by law."

The wishes and the aspirations of the Belgian hierarchy in this matter were expressed in a letter of the Archbishop of Malines, Prince de Méan, to the members of the National Congress, which letter was read to them by their President, Baron Surlet de Chokier (1769-1839), on December 17, 1830.[17] The Archbishop made a request to the Assembly that full and complete liberty be guaranteed to the Church, not only in theory, as the Dutch government had done, but also in practice.

The great importance of this episcopal intervention rests in the fact that, here for the first time in Belgian history, a responsible Churchman renounced all privileges of the "old regime." All the Church wanted was to see its members sharing in that complete liberty that should be the privilege of all citizens. Practically for the Catholic Church this meant never to be hindered or restricted in the exercise of its religious functions; to be free and independent in its internal regime, particularly in the nomination of the clergy and the relations with the Holy See; to possess the right of association and peaceable assembly.

The content of this letter proves by itself how unjust it is to describe this intervention of the Archbishop as an unwarranted encroachment on the domain of the State. In writing this letter to the National Congress Archbishop de Méan acted only as a citizen using the right of petition. And the fact that in this letter the prelate also requested that the State provide financial support for the clergy was not only justified by the social rôle of the clergy of any denomination whatsoever, but especially as a compensation to the Catholic clergy for church property unjustly confiscated under the French regime.

Considering freedom of education as a necessary safeguard

---

[17] This letter was almost like the last will of the Archbishop. He died the next month, on January 13, 1831. Cf. Demarteau, *François-Antoine de Méan, dernier Prince-Évêque de Liège, premier Primat de Belgique* (Bruxelles: Office de Publicité, 1944).

for freedom of religion, and remembering too well the sad experience of the Dutch school legislation, the Archbishop wrote in his letter: "As religion is so intimately and closely allied with instruction, religion would not be free if instruction were not free." His proposal therefore was: "full and complete liberty in teaching, to the exclusion of any preventing measure." His special request was that Congress would "lay down specifically that institutions for the training to the priesthood be placed exclusively under the direction and supervision of the ecclesiastical authorities."[18]

Intended to be the basic directive for the future religious and educational policy of the new State, this letter should not have left open any way for misunderstanding or double interpretation. Of course, the discussions in the Assembly show that in the Catholic mind of 1830 freedom of instruction for Catholics could not be restricted to the free education of the clergy. But, the text itself of this episcopal letter, taken out of its historical circumstances, was later to be interpreted by the Liberals as if only the seminaries had to be under the direction and the supervision of the Church, while all other Catholic schools had to admit supervision and at least partial direction by the State.[19]

Art. 13 of the draft-constitution made the following provision: "Instruction is free; all measures preventing this are forbidden. The measures for supervision and repression shall be regulated by law. Public instruction given at the expense of the State shall likewise be regulated by law."

The public discussion in the Congress on December 24, 1830, brought out the scepticism of the Catholic members about the feasibility of this proposal. Of course, its text proclaimed freedom of instruction. But, the memory of the Dutch Fundamental

---

[18] ". . . comme la religion a une connexion si intime et si nécessaire avec l'enseignement . . . elle ne saurait être libre si l'enseignement ne l'est aussi." . . . "la liberté pleine et entière de l'enseignement; il écartera, à cet effet, toute mesure préventive. . . ." ". . . de stipuler spécialement que les établissements consacrés à l'instruction et à l'éducation des jeunes gens destinés au service des autels seront placés exclusivement sous la direction et la surveillance des supérieurs ecclésiastiques." Cf. Simon, *Le Cardinal Sterckx et son Temps,* I, p. 143.

[19] Cf. Simon, *op. cit.,* I, p. 143.

Law with all its theoretical freedoms was still too vivid to make the Catholics accept a liberty combined with supervision from the State. Not only preventing measures, but also that inspection by the State would never be accepted again.

Although agreement on the principle of educational freedom was easily attained among Catholics and Liberals, the differences on State control over religious schools almost led to the breaking of the "Union of the Opposition." Catholics feared State monopoly, Liberals feared Church monopoly. Knowing that many Catholic members had already left for the religious holidays, the Liberals forced the vote on this on Christmas eve, 1830, in the hope that they could impose their own views by gaining a majority in a snap vote which would enable them to outnumber the Catholics. This unfair maneuver did not succeed anyhow. By 76 votes to 71 the National Congress rejected all State supervision over the schools, and sanctioned the most unlimited freedom in the field of education. The amended art. 13 of the draft-proposal became art. 17 of the Constitution. No authorization or license is necessary to open a school; absolute freedom in the selection of method and curriculum; and especially no State inspection of any kind.[20]

It is evident that this extremist attitude of the National Congress was first of all a vivid reaction against the former Dutch school system. The fear for the re-introduction of the hated Dutch district-inspector explains particularly the rejection of any kind of State supervision whatsoever. But, even in the midst of violent debates the Catholic members of the constituent assembly found time to point out the philosophical bases of this unlimited freedom of education. In their minds freedom of education was only the logical consequence of the already guaranteed freedom of religion.[21] This was particularly true in regard to the training of the young clergy, while the claim for educational freedom for

[20] Cf. Huyttens de Terbecq, *Discussions du Congrès National de Belgique, 1830-1831* (2 vols., Bruxelles: Société typographique belge, 1844-1845), I, pp. 625-642.

[21] "Comme nous voulons la liberté des cultes et de la presse, nous voulons aussi la liberté de l'enseignement; l'une aujourd'hui ne saurait subsister sans l'autre."—Van Crombrugghe. Cf. Huyttens, *op. cit.*, I, p. 634.

all other schools was always first based upon the primary rights of the family. "If monopoly must be avoided in everything, this is above all true where there is question of restricting the rights of paternal authority."[22] To advocate freedom of instruction, to demand for the father of a family the right to choose the one to whom he will entrust the destiny of his children, was for the members of the National Congress nothing but demanding that parents be not prevented from exercising their natural prerogatives and using their inalienable rights.[23]

May one go so far as to assume that in the Belgian Constitution the educational rôle of the State is only secondary and merely subsidiary? The answer is absolutely affirmative. An objective study of the discussions of the National Congress permits the following interpretation of art. 17.

The civil authority has no obligation at all to open and to direct schools of its own as long as the parents, directly or indirectly, provide the necessary education for their children. In theory, however, the civil authority has the same right as each individual to make use of the constitutional freedom of instruction and to open its own schools. But, the practical application of this theoretical right was hardly conceivable in the minds of the Belgians of 1830, who never thought of any education in their Catholic country that would not be religious and therefore not directed by the Church. What is more, in order to close the door against any State monopoly or unfair suppression of private initiative, the second part of art. 17 states that even the public instruction given

---

[22] "Si l'on doit éviter soigneusement le monopole en toute chose, c'est surtout quand il s'agit de restreindre les droits résultants de l'autorité paternelle, que le pouvoir doit examiner avec soin et défiance, si les dispositions qu'il croit devoir prendre sont impérieusement commandées par le bien-être général de la société."—Dams. Cf. Huyttens, *op. cit.,* I, p. 629.

[23] "En réclamant la liberté de l'enseignement, en demandant pour la famille les garanties de la concurrence, le libre droit du père de choisir celui entre les mains duquel il veut confier les destinées de son fils, que demandons-nous sinon qu'on n'empêche pas les parents d'user d'une prérogative naturelle, d'un droit imprescreptible, qui d'ailleurs ne leur fut guère disputé que par un Julien l'apostat, un Robespierre, un Van Maanen."—Van Crombrugghe. Cf. Huyttens, *op. cit.,* I, p. 634.

at the expense of the State is to be regulated, not by the government, but by a law sanctioned by a parliamentary majority.

The Liberal opinion, that the Constitution makes it obligatory for the State to have its own neutral schools in all circumstances, is just a typical example of one putting the ideas of a Liberal majority of 1880 into the minds of a Catholic majority of 1830. Even if art. 17 of the Constitution was accepted by only a majority of five votes, as long as this Constitution has not been amended in the legally provided way, the elementary rules of legal security will always call for the application and interpretation of this fundamental law in accordance with the views of those who first sanctioned it.[24]

This purely subsidiary rôle of the State in educational matters was decisively confirmed by the fact that for the next ten years the whole of the primary instruction in the country was confined to the Church-directed Catholic schools and the schools directed by private citizens. The only "public instruction given at the expense of the State" was the instruction given in Catholic schools subsidized by the government.

In the following chapter it will be seen that this unlimited liberty and the exclusion of all control by the State led to deplorable abuses. But, to pass judgment on the results of the application of a fundamental principle is one thing; to admit the historical fact that a certain constitutional principle, good or bad, was laid down is quite another thing. And as far as this last point goes, it is considered abundantly clear that the majority of the constituents of 1830 wanted to reduce the educational rôle of the State to zero. Reacting against the extreme of the Dutch system they ended up in the opposite extreme. It was to take them but ten years to find out that the old saying, *"in medio stat virtus,"* could still be applied to public education in a modern State, even when the State is one that holds an overwhelming Catholic majority.

---

[24] For the Liberal viewpoint see Juste, *Le Congrès National de Belgique, 1830-1831* (2 vols., Bruxelles: C. Muquardt, 1880), I, p. 363.

CHAPTER V

The Compromise Law of 1842

In consequence of a continued spirit of unity among all citizens the first governments of Belgium were able to devote all their energy to the internal organization of the new State. Of particular importance for the future school system were the laws of 1836 concerning the organization of communes and provinces.

Adhering to the best traditions of local autonomy, the *Communal Law* of March 30, 1836, gave almost complete self-government to the individual communities.[1] All communes, numbering 2,670 at the present day, are administered by a "communal council" elected by the people, and by a "college of burgomaster and aldermen" appointed by the King.[2] The burgomaster possesses executive power and draws up the police regulations. The aldermen have in their charge the different administrative branches. The communal council discusses and votes on all matters of interest to the community, prepares its budget, and is entitled to levy certain taxes.

According to the *Provincial Law* of April 30, 1836, each of the nine Belgian provinces is directed by a "provincial council" directly elected by the people but having far less autonomy than the communal councils, yet exercising similar functions. When the provincial council is not in session, authority is vested in a permanent body of at least six "deputies." The governor, appointed by the King, is the representative of the executive power. In county administration the commissioners have no autonomy at all, but are merely the agents of the provincial government. While both the communal and the provincial authorities possess legislative and executive power, they do not have any judicial power. However,

---

[1] Cf. Van Haesendonck, *De juiste Teksten van de Belgische Grondwet, van de Gemeentewet, en van de Provinciale Wet* (Brussel: E. Guyot, 1948).

[2] The law of December 30, 1887, left to the King only the nomination of the burgomaster, while the aldermen were to be elected by the communal council.

while each commune constitutes a direct autonomous governmental entity, and as such is directly representative of the voting people, the provinces are mere intermediary branches between the communes and the central government.

This *Central Government* has legislative, executive, and judicial power. The *legislative power* is exercised by the King jointly with the two houses of Parliament, the Chamber of Representatives and the Senate, the members of which are chosen by the people in direct, secret and frequent elections. The *executive power* is exercised by the King through his ministers whose principal function it is to assume responsibility for the acts of the King. In fact, except for purely military decisions made by the King in his capacity as commander-in-chief of the armed forces, no act of the King can be put into effect unless it is countersigned by a responsible minister (art. 64 of the Constitution). This explains why the King can never be held responsible for legal acts and why his person is inviolable (art. 63 of the Constitution). Even article 65 of the Constitution, stating that the King appoints and dismisses his ministers, must be understood in the same sense as the British parliamentary system, namely: a minister remains in power only as long as he enjoys the confidence of a majority in Parliament which keeps the executive power in check by means of the annual vote on the public budget (art. 115 of the Constitution). As regards *judicial power* in Belgium, judges, once appointed by the King through his responsible minister, are irremovable (art. 99 and 100 of the Constitution).

Though the internal organization of the new State was thus stabilized, the country still had to go through three more years of tension and diplomatic negotiations before the treaties recognizing the Belgian independence were signed at London on April 19, 1839, by all the interested parties.[8]

It seemed as if the Belgian Catholics and Liberals had been waiting for this precise moment to break up their marriage of convenience. As soon as it became evident that the international status of the nation was stabilized the internal cohesion between

---

[8] Cf. de Lannoy-Fleury, *Histoire diplomatique de l'Indépendance belge, 1830-1839* (Bruxelles: Office de Publicité, 1948).

the citizens no longer seemed essential, and all the old latent differences reappeared immediately.

From the very beginning of their "union of the opposition" Catholics and Liberals had always had a different conception of that liberty that had become their common battle-slogan. Catholics fought for liberty as a means to make their religion strong and influential; Liberals wanted liberty in order to put an end to all Church-influence on the public life of the nation.

An episcopal directive on December 28, 1837, stating that the lodges of Freemasons in Belgium came under the pontifical condemnations of secret societies and that therefore no member of the Catholic Church should belong to them, widened the breach between Left and Right.[4] Discussions as to whether candidates for the priesthood should be exempt from or subject to military service caused yet another upset in 1838 and 1839. The gap between Catholics and Liberals grew even wider in the following three years, when the question of the juridical status of the Catholic University of Louvain was raised.[5] This continued friction finally brought about the rupture of the "Union of the Opposition."[6] And although the Catholic-Liberal coalition was only publicly broken by the Liberal electoral victory of June 8, 1847, the spirit of the union of 1828 was definitely gone when on April 13, 1841, the cabinet of Joseph Lebeau (1796-1862) resigned.[7] This is the

[4] Leo XII in his encyclical *Quo graviora mala* (1825) confirmed Benedict XIV's condemnation of Freemasonry and of other secret societies. In view of the necessary royal "placet" under the former governments these pontifical decisions had only partially been published in the Belgian provinces. Consequently, many Belgians, Catholics as well as Liberals, still believed that the Belgian masonic lodges were just benevolent and philanthropical societies, not at all condemned by the Church. Cf. Berteloot, *La Franc-maçonnerie et l'Église catholique* (2 vols., Paris: Collection Hommes et Cités, 1945); Quigley, *Condemned Societies* (Washington, D. C.: The Catholic University of America, 1927).

[5] Founded in 1425 by papal bull of Martin V at the request of the Duke of Brabant, John IV, the Catholic University had been reopened in 1834. Cf. van der Essen, *L'Université de Louvain, 1425-1940* (Bruxelles: Éditions universitaires, 1945).

[6] Cf. Simon, *Le Cardinal Sterckx et son Temps*, I, pp. 319-364.

[7] Cf. Lebeau, *Souvenirs personnels, 1824-1841, et Correspondance diplomatique* (Bruxelles, 1883).

reason why, in the writer's opinion, the first law organizing the elementary schools in Belgium should not be called a law of unity, "une loi unioniste," but rather a law of compromise.

Strange as it may seem, the very idea of a law that would organize the primary education in the country was not at all acceptable to most Belgian Catholics of those days. It was only in a spirit of obedience and loyalty that finally Catholic opinion allied itself with the views of Archbishop Engelbert Sterckx (1792-1867) and Premier Jean-Baptiste de Nothomb (1805-1881) who were the great champions of this law. Yet, the true need for some kind of law concerning the elementary schools in Belgium after the first decade of its independence can hardly be denied. The real conditions called for some legal intervention, and so-called juridical objections had no legal value.

There can be no question that the violent reaction against the Dutch school system had resulted in the replacing of one abuse by another. Unlimited freedom of instruction had brought the country from an authoritarian State-controlled system to an almost chaotic educational condition. Since the influence of the civil authorities was restricted to the subsidized schools, the entire primary educational system was left in the hands of the individual citizens. There is no doubt that the number of schools and teachers had been increasing steadily since the revolution, as unlimited freedom of instruction meant that everyone, qualified or not, had the right to set himself up as a public teacher.[8] The qualifications of such improvised teachers and also their "educational methods" often transcended the realm of the imaginable.[9] The lack of sufficient training schools for teachers was the principal reason why in 1838 the annual report of the various provincial authorities revealed that two thirds of the country's teachers had never given any legal proof of their qualifications. No wonder that in such

---

[8] Impressed by the numerical strength of the schools some authors have nothing but praise for the Belgian elementary school system between 1830 and 1840. Thus Verhaegen, *De Schoolstrijd in Belgie* (Sottegem: Eylenbosch & Dupon, 1906), p. 10, who furthermore notes that of the 5,189 elementary schools in 1840, 2,284 were completely administered and supported by the Catholic ecclesiastical authorities.

[9] Cf. Van Kalken, *Histoire de Belgique des Origines à 1914*, p. 552.

conditions many parents did not even bother to send their children to any school at all. Hence it was that Belgium, while being among the leading industrial countries of the European continent, occupied a humiliating back-seat in the field of popular education.[10]

To remedy these undeniable defects of the elementary educational system a law was already drafted and introduced in 1834, but neither Catholics nor Liberals accepted it. For more than seven years discussions over the pros and cons of that law went on. Most Liberals then rejected any school law because they saw no possibility of the present Catholic majority ever sanctioning the Liberal ideal of State controlled neutral education. Catholics, who up to then had *de facto* at least, a school monopoly in most localities, were afraid that any State intervention would weaken this privileged position. This was the real reason for Catholic and Liberal opposition to a school law. The juridical arguments invoked by them to bolster their strategical position do not seem of a very solid nature.

Was it really an offense against the freedom of instruction guaranteed in the Constitution to accept a law organizing the primary education in the country? It seems not. The text of art. 17 of the Constitution itself refers to some kind of State intervention, when it mentions that the public instruction given at the expense of the State is to be regulated by law. Even if the rôle of the State in educational matters had to be purely secondary according to the Constitution, the above mentioned defects in the educational

---

[10] Cf. Ducpétiaux, *Quelques Mots sur l'État actuel de l'Instruction primaire en Belgique, et sur la Nécessité de l'améliorer* (Bruxelles: de Weissenbruch, 1839), pp. 11-12, who gives the following statistics: With a population of 4,225,783 Belgium had only 422,488 pupils in its elementary schools, an average of 1 pupil for every 10 inhabitants. Many American states, particularly the state of New York, had then already 1 elementary school pupil for every 4 inhabitants, while in Europe Belgium's low standing was only surpassed by the even worse situation in Britain (1 for every 11), in Lombardy (1 for every 12.6), in Ireland (1 for every 13.2), and in France (1 for every 13.3). Cf. also de Nothomb, *État de l'Instruction primaire en Belgique, 1830-1840* (Bruxelles, 1842); *Rapport décennal sur la Situation de l'Instruction primaire en Belgique, 1830-1840* (Bruxelles: Ministère de l'Intérieur, 1842); Thiersch, *Über den gegenwärtigen Zustand des öffentlichen Unterrichts in . . . Belgien* (3 vols., Stuttgart, 1838).

system called for the intervention of the civil authorities, not indeed to take over the work of the parents and the Church, but to co-ordinate and to perfect their efforts for the technical development of the school system and the greatest common welfare of society.[11] How up to 1842 Catholics and Liberals could still be discussing the principle of a badly needed State intervention in the field of primary education seems beyond comprehension. Six years earlier this same principle had already been accepted in the law of September 27, 1835, whereby two State universities were created without any real necessity for them, for the Catholic University of Louvain and the Liberal University of Brussels were more than sufficient for the moral and intellectual needs of a free country.[12]

If not the Constitution, was the traditional independence of the local communities, as sanctioned in the communal law of 1836, to be the legal obstacle to a central school legislation? Many thought so in those days. To them local civil authorities had the right, like all individual citizens, to claim the constitutional freedom of instruction, and consequently to run their schools in complete independence. Yet, however legitimate and efficient this local autonomy could be in several fields, in modern society public instruction could hardly be looked upon as a matter of purely domestic importance.[13]

But, above all, Catholics feared that any legislation about elementary schools would be the first step to a return of the old

[11] Cf. the first part of this study, especially pp. 19-23.

[12] Ducpétiaux (*op. cit.*, p. 13) noted *ad rem*: "Ce qu'on a fait il y a quatre ans dans l'intérêt des classes aisées et de l'enseignement supérieur, pourquoi ne le ferait-on pas aujourd'hui dans l'intérêt des classes bourgeoises et ouvrières et de l'enseignement primaire et moyen? On a interverti l'ordre naturel des choses; on a commencé par où l'on aurait dû finir; à la rigueur on aurait pu abandonner l'enseignement supérieur à lui-même . . . mais il n'en est pas de même des écoles moyennes et primaires. . . ."

[13] The words of Guizot in the French Parliament on March 24, 1837, can be applied to any country: "L'Instruction publique est partout d'intérêt général; elle n'est point comme les questions de propriété, comme les questions de petite voirie, renfermée dans le cercle des intérêts purements locaux. . . . Tout ce qui est d'intérêt général . . . est du ressort . . . de la puissance centrale. . . . Qu'on réclame la liberté pour les individus, oui, mais pas pour les conseils municipaux pour tout ce qui est d'intérêt général."—Quoted by Ducpétiaux, *op. cit.*, pp. 14-15.

Dutch monopoly-system and to the final abolition of true freedom of religion. This fear of most Catholics, including the bishops, finally disappeared when in 1839 Archbishop Sterckx succeeded in winning them over to his views.

In his "Draft-proposal to be sent to the Legislature" Sterckx sought to prove that a school system can be truly organized without the jeopardizing, in any way, of the freedom of religion. He based his reasoning on the old principle of the Constituent Assembly that freedom of religion calls for freedom of instruction. Besides that, like most men in Europe in those days, Sterckx could not even think of education that would not be religious. At the same time seeing that Belgium was still ninety per cent Catholic, he felt that a religious education there could only mean a Catholic education.[14]

From these principles, agreed upon by the government, Sterckx drew some practical conclusions that the State was not going to accept so easily: ecclesiastical supervision of the whole of public instruction, and intervention in the nomination and revocation of teachers.

To Sterckx all this seemed very logical. Freedom of religion, sanctioned in the Constitution, required the recognition of the Constitution of the Catholic Church. And, according to the law of the Church, the bishops existed as the official teachers of religion, and thus were the only ones who could appoint those who in their name were to teach the Catholic religion in the schools. Furthermore, since true religious education meant that all branches of instruction were to be imbued with the religious spirit, Sterckx thought that no teacher should be appointed without the consent of the local pastor who, as the bishop's delegate, not only directed the formal religious and moral courses, but supervised the whole education.

After three more years of endless discussions among Catholics and Liberals the first Belgian law organizing primary education

---

[14] It is worthwhile to note that in asserting this right to a Catholic education in the Belgian schools the archbishop did not base his claim on a dogmatical basis, but merely invoked the constitutional freedom for all religions. Cf. Simon, *Le Cardinal Sterckx et son Temps,* I, pp. 375-381.

was passed in the Chamber of Representatives on August 30, 1842, with only three Liberals voting against it and one abstention. It was unanimously approved in the Senate on September 21, and received the enthusiastic sanction of the King on September 23.[15]

This law became the charter of the Belgian primary school system for 37 years, to be complemented later on with royal ordinances and ministerial instructions, and even today some of its fundamental principles are invoked in the Belgian school legislation.

Its 37 articles can be reduced to these principal demands: Each commune had to have at least one public school in its territory, but the local civil authorities could either recognize and make use of an existing private or denominational school, or build their own public school. The commune selected the teachers from the ranks of the graduates of either the State-administered or the State-recognized "normal schools," and alone, without any ecclesiastical intervention, gave them their appointments. The commune also assumed full responsibility for school expenses, but received subsidies from the provincial and central government. The right of inspection belonged to the commune itself and to the State-inspectors, but the ecclesiastical authorities could exercise complete supervision over the books used for religious and moral instruction. Instruction was always free for needy children. Religious and moral instruction were a compulsory part of the school curriculum in all public schools; this instruction was given by the regular teacher himself under the supervision of the Church and according to his own religious belief and that of the majority of the pupils; children belonging to another religion were exempted from this formal religious course.[16]

To pass a judgment on this law of 1842 is no easy task. A critical study of the parliamentary discussions on the official text and of the later applications of the law has led the writer to the conclusion that this compromise-law should not have received the support of the Catholics, since it was from the outset nothing else than a political trap which would necessarily prove fatal to them.

---

[15] Cf. Bronne, *Léopold Ier et son Temps* (Bruxelles: A. Goemaere, 1942).

[16] Cf. Alvin, *Discussion sur la Loi de l'Instruction primaire du 23 septembre 1842* (Bruxelles, 1843).

Before the law was even voted on, the way for its future confusing and conflicting interpretation was laid wide open by Premier de Nothomb himself. The same text was explained by him privately to the bishops as being entirely favorable to the Catholics, while publicly in Parliament he asserted that it was perfectly acceptable to the Liberals. What then would be more logical than that private unofficial explanations be easily forgotten and that only the public interpretations be kept in the official records?

And, no doubt, in the public discussion of the law the Liberals wrung out of de Nothomb one concession after the other. The teachers in the civil public schools were to be appointed only by the communal council without any ecclesiastical intervention at all. The Catholic religion, the religion of nine tenths of the population, did not enjoy any privileged position, but was treated like any other religion. The Catholic doctrine, it is true, was generally to be taught in all the public schools and under the supervision of the clergy, but any eventual absence of such Church-intervention never sufficed to affect the legal existence of a public school. First de Nothomb had explained that the "confessional" character of the civil public school was so essential, that whenever the clergy would cease to co-operate with a school, such a school would legally no longer exist. Immediately he tried to reassure the Liberals that the clergy would always be sensible in using its rights. The next concession was this: abuses alleged by the clergy to justify their disapproval of a certain school would have legal consequences only if verified and accepted by the government. The last step, however, was the acceptance of the Liberal view, namely that a public school could still legally continue its existence without any relations whatsoever with the clergy.

At the time of all these successive capitulations de Nothomb was still assuring the Catholic hierarchy of the confessional character and the truly religious atmosphere that would always pervade the civil public elementary school!

Was it surprising that, up to the last minute, outstanding Catholic political leaders such as Adolphe Dechamps (1807-1875) and Philippe de Mérode (1791-1857), backed by most bishops and priests, opposed this law? When they finally, in spirit of discipline, bowed to the views of Archbishop Sterckx, the future Minister Dechamps expressed the common feelings of the Catholic majority, by his prophetical words: "The day will come when they will regret it."[17]

Does all this mean that one's judgment on this law must eventuate in a condemnation of both Premier de Nothomb and Archbishop Sterckx as being the spiritual fathers of this law?[18]

A distinction between de Nothomb and Sterckx is here necessary. Without questioning the sincerity of de Nothomb's religious convictions and his efficient statesmanship in other fields, in the elaboration of the school law of 1842 he appeared rather as the shifty politician. Hopelessly trying to turn back the hands of time, de Nothomb was ready to go to the extreme in compromising, if only the Catholic-Liberal coalition could be kept alive. In his opinion, the very existence of the nation in an internationally troubled world depended completely on the maintenance of the old "Union of the Opposition."

The future history, however, was to prove that Belgium would still be going along in the world after this Catholic-Liberal coalition was definitely gone. And in what regards the internal-political viewpoint, a statesman like de Nothomb should have known how the Liberal mind of 1842 differed from that of 1828; he should also have realized that his own Catholic premiership would not last forever and that this law, once in Liberal hands, would become fatal to the Catholic school system, as was expressed in a truly realistic way by the Liberal Veydt, on August 28, 1842, when he said: "I find the law sufficiently complete . . . thanks to the explanations that had to be given regarding its application; and the law will leave nothing to be desired, once it is in the hands of a Liberal government; and that will have to come about, one day."[19]

---

[17] Cf. de Moreau, *Adolphe Dechamps, 1807-1875* (Bruxelles: A. Dewit, 1911); Simon, *Le Cardinal Sterckx et son Temps,* I, pp. 390-393.

[18] Simon (*op. cit.,* p. 400) gives almost the whole "credit" for this law to Archbishop Sterckx whom he furthermore with love and admiration tries to excuse for having accepted the lesser evil in those days.

[19] "Je trouve la loi assez complète . . . grâce aux explications que l'on a été forcé de donner sur son exécution; et celle-ci laissera peu de chose à

Should a similar judgment be passed on Archbishop Sterckx in this matter? Unfortunately, yes. This was the conclusion the writer reached the very first time he studied from the viewpoint of Canon Law this particular period of Belgium's history. The later reading of Simon's solid work on "Cardinal Sterckx and his time" has not forced him in any way to whittle down his opinion.

Should it accordingly be said that, to save the political unity of his country, the thirteenth Archbishop of Malines sacrificed the interests of his Church?[20] Not at all. The saintly high-priest Sterckx was always too well aware of his great responsibilities ever to permit himself to become what a great historian once called the worst of all priestly deviations, the prelate-politician.[21]

The only trouble with Sterckx was that his whole background and experience had made him a living anachronism in the Belgium of the nineteenth century. His whole mind was still impregnated with the spirit of the old regime when separation between Church and State was just inconceivable. Although the Belgian Constitution did no longer admit the union between Church and State, in the mind of Sterckx the Catholic religion was still *de facto* the religion of the country. He regarded working for his country as working for his Church and vice versa, since he could never envisage any conflict between his ecclesiastical duties and his civic obligations. He looked on himself, as did the medieval bishops before him, as the *defensor civitatis,* the shepherd constantly worrying about unity among all citizens. Sterckx's optimistic belief in the fundamental honesty of his political opponents almost matched his confidence in the lasting power of Catholicity in Belgium.

This optimism, however, reached the stage of political naïveté in his acceptance of the school law of 1842. He must have known

---

désirer lorsqu'elle sera confiée à un ministère libéral, ce qui arrivera fatalement un jour."—Cf. Discailles, *Charles Rogier* (4 vols., Bruxelles: A. Dewit, 1892-1895), III, p. 79.

[20] Even Simon (*Le Cardinal Sterckx et son Temps,* I, p. 400), notwithstanding all his admiration for Sterckx, seems to insinuate this when he writes: "En supposant que, eu regard des intérêts catholiques, il ait eu tort de protéger cette loi, l'on comprend qu'il ait voulu à l'origine de notre vie politique continuer l'union qui avait présidé à notre révolution."

[21] de Reynold, *L'Europe tragique* (Paris: Ed. Spes, 1934), p. 206.

that the confusing text of the law itself left the way open for dangerous interpretations. But, in his mind no government in a Catholic country could ever dare to apply this law against the Church of the immense majority. On the contrary, for Sterckx this law could make the Catholic education the official education of the Belgian civil public school, and thus relieve the Church of the material and financial burden of maintaining its own school system.

And here precisely was the tragic mistake of Archbishop Sterckx: by seeking to bring all civil public schools into the hands of the Church, he left the way open for that Church to lose its own schools. Taking their stand with Sterckx and from then on considering all civil public schools as potential Catholic schools, bishops, priests and Catholic lay people renounced that initiative that had caused them within the last ten years to erect 2,284 schools. If he had lived long enough, Cardinal Sterckx would have seen that in thirty-five years the application of "his" law brought the number of independent Catholic schools down to 958, while during the same period the number of civil public schools increased from 2,109 to 4,157.[22] And as regards "Catholic" education in those civil public schools, suffice it to quote a historian, who wrote: "In the course of the years the law of 1842 had lost its confessional character in the big cities. The teaching body there was atheistic; the crucifix had disappeared from the classrooms; religious teaching had given place to a course in gymnastics."[23] The "administrative corrections" of the law, predicted by the Liberals, had been very effective. Precisely what Sterckx had wanted to avoid by accepting the law of 1842 had become a sad reality: thousands of Catholic children were left without religious education in their schools. It was then, but too late, that the

---

[22] Cf. Baudouin, *Rapport sur l'État actuel de l'Enseignement spécial et de l'Enseignement primaire en Belgique, en Allemagne, et en Suisse* (Paris: Imprimerie impériale, 1865).; Sauveur, *Royaume de Belgique. Etat intellectuel* (Bruxelles: Commission centrale de Statistique, 1876).

[23] "Au cours des années, la loi de 1842 avait perdu son caractère confessionel dans les grandes villes. Le corps enseignant y était athée; les crucifix avaient disparus des classes; l'enseignement de la religion avait été remplacé par un cours de gymnastique."—Van Kalken, *La Belgique contemporaine,* p. 119.

Catholics realized the full import of Dechamps' prophetic warning against turning the Catholic school system over to a government that some day might become antireligious.[24]

But, should not we rather mitigate our judgment on Archbishop Sterckx by admitting that in this particular matter the circumstances did not leave any other alternative?[25] By no means. There was definitely another possibility. On one hand the State should have taken the necessary legal measures to remedy the technical defects of the existing educational system; and here Sterckx was certainly right in invoking the necessity of some law. But, on the other hand, Sterckx should have done what other bishops and Catholic lay leaders wanted, namely, to continue the concentration of all Catholic forces for the expansion of the existing Catholic school system. Here again the writer subscribes to the views of the Liberal historian Van Kalken who, objectively judging the case, wrote: "The Belgian clergy would have been powerful enough, if they desired, to bring to naught the efforts of the government."[26] And answering the objection that in 1842 the Belgian Catholics were not sufficiently organized and financially equipped for such an enterprise, we point to what they were able to do in 1879-1884, with a better organization, of course, but in far worse circumstances.

---

[24] Cf. de Moreau, *L'Église en Belgique des Origines au Début du XXe Siècle,* p. 233.

[25] Simon mildly insinuates this thesis in his *Le Cardinal Sterckx et son Temps,* I, p. 399.

[26] "Le clergé belge aurait été assez puissant pour réduire à néant, s'il l'eut voulu, l'effort du ministère."—*La Belgique contemporaine,* p. 119.

CHAPTER VI

The Law of Misfortune (1879)

It was certainly a far cry from the days of the union of 1828 to June 14, 1846, when the Liberal Congress of Brussels manifested its intention to fight for a so-called "real independence of the civil power in all domains." With regard to the educational field the same congress proclaimed the necessity of "organizing public instruction in all its degrees under the exclusive direction of the civil authorities, . . . with the rejection of all authoritative intervention of the clergy in any civil public school."

A year later, on August 12, 1847, Charles Rogier (1800-1885) formed a homogeneous Liberal cabinet to make this party-program a political reality. From then on, frictions between the Church and the Liberal government became commonplace in Belgium's public life. Reacting against the progressing secularization of society, Catholics on their side organized forces in the first Congresses of Malines in 1863 and 1864.[1] When nevertheless, after a Catholic interregnum of eight years, the elections of June 11, 1878, brought a new victory for the Liberals, the stage was set for the most bitter fight the Church had yet to wage: the fight for "the soul of the child."

One of the first acts of the new Liberal majority was the creation of a separate and distinct Ministry of Public Instruction, that up to then had been under the control of the Ministry of the Interior. The philosophical orientation of the new department became immediately evident when the position of Minister of Public Instruction was entrusted to the fanatical freemason Pieter Van Humbeeck who already in 1864 had made himself famous by a speech in which he referred to the Catholic Church as "that corpse of days gone by." Here now was the right man in the right place

---

[1] Cf. *Assemblée générale des Catholiques en Belgique* (5 vols., Bruxelles, 1864-1868); Simon, *Le Cardinal Sterckx et son Temps,* I, pp. 545-609; Van Kalken, *Histoire de Belgique,* pp. 550-551.

to execute most slavishly the orders given by the freemasons' Grand Orient which especially since 1850 had come out openly with the slogan: "The priest out of the school!"[2]

If the Liberals of 1878 had not been so intoxicated by their electoral success, they would have thought twice before attempting the so-called "revision of the school-law of 1842." Successive Liberal governments had already watered down the confessional character of this law to such an extent that, at least in the cities, the civil public school had become what the freemasons wanted it to be: "a school without God."[3] But, no; the Grand-Orient wanted more: an open declaration of principles, and the extension of the "progressive school" to the smallest country-village in the nation.[4] The mistake made forty years earlier by Archbishop Sterckx was now to be repeated by Minister Van Humbeeck. Just as Sterckx lost his own Catholic institutions by trying to take over all civil public schools, so now by attempting to eliminate all religious schools Van Humbeeck was to ruin the civil public school system.

Up to the last moment the Belgian hierarchy had prudently observed a rather watchful but conciliatory attitude. However, when the speech-from-the-throne at the opening of the parliamentary year 1878-1879 took up again the program of the Liberal Congress of 1846, by stating that "public instruction must be exclusively under the civil authority," the bishops were forced to accept the challenge.

Quite the opposite to what had happened in 1842, now the Archbishop, Victor Cardinal Dechamps (1810-1883), did not stand alone, but was backed unanimously by all the bishops, priests and Catholic lay leaders of the country. In a joint pastoral letter of December 7, 1878, the Belgian bishops challenged the Liberal attacks against the Church by pointing out the many services the Church had rendered to the civil society, especially in the educa-

---

[2] Cf. Dechamps, *Les Projets inconstitutionnels contre la Loi de 1842* (Bruxelles: 1878); Maillie, *La Maçonnerie belge d'après les Documents maçonniques* (Bruxelles, 1906); Verhaegen, *De Schoolstrijd in Belgie* (Sottegem, 1906).

[3] Cf. supra, p. 73.

[4] Van Kalken, *Histoire de Belgique*, p. 553.

tional field. The suppression of religious instruction in civil public schools was depicted as contrary not only to the divine law and the moral and social needs of the nation, but also to both the letter and the spirit of the Constitution and the justified wishes of the majority of the population.[5]

But, no episcopal protest could sidetrack the Liberals from what they thought to be the road to victory. On January 21, 1879, a belated Christmas-present was offered to the nation by the Liberal draft-proposal of a new school law. Carefully studied, the 50 articles of the proposed law presented these two characteristics: complete secularization of education, and supreme educational jurisdiction of the central government.

The complete secularization of education was sanctioned in art. 4, that "left religious instruction to the families and the ministers of the different religions," and in art. 5, that replaced religious instruction in the schools with a form of instruction based upon a so-called "common morality," which was to be imparted by the teacher under the exclusive direction and supervision of the governmental officials. But, to keep up an appearance of friendliness towards the Catholic population, the second paragraph of art. 4 provided that in the civil public school a classroom would be at the disposal of the religious ministers who outside the regular school hours could there instruct the pupils of their own denomination. In case the Catholic clergy would refuse to provide such religious instruction, the teacher himself would be allowed, if he wanted to, to teach verbatim the official catechism text without explanation of any kind. Far from being compulsory, however, such extracurricular religious instruction could only be attended

[5] Let it be noted that in those days even a parliamentary majority was not always an adequate expression of public opinion in the nation, for till 1894 the right to vote in Belgium was conditioned on the payment of a certain amount of taxes and thus was restricted to the wealthy classes. Only in the elections of 1894 a wider formula, the so-called "plural suffrage-system," was adopted. While every male citizen was then entitled to vote for the members of the legislature, still a second and even a third vote was accorded to citizens who held certain properties or who possessed a certificate of higher studies. Immediately after the first World-War really universal and equal male-suffrage was introduced: one man, one vote. The country had to go through a second World-War before the same franchise was extended to women.

by pupils whose parents had explicitly requested so.[6] And to make sure that such religious instruction would not run counter to the general "education" of the child, art. 7 and art. 43 stated that thenceforth to teach in civil public schools one had to be a graduate from the State-administered "normal schools," where all religious education was excluded.

The supreme jurisdiction of the central government in educational matters was already expressed in art. 1 of the proposed law, compelling every local community to have at least one such official and irreligious school in its territory, regardless of whether or not the population wanted such a school. Art. 2 furthermore authorized the central government to determine the exact number of schools, classes and teachers, needed in each local community. The right for the communal authorities to recognize and make use of existing private or denominational schools, as sanctioned in the law of 1842, was abolished (art. 46). Almost returning completely to the old Dutch State monopoly the central government reserved for itself the whole right of school inspection (art. 23). It even revived the old Dutch "local committees" which were supposed to supervise the public instruction in the community, but which in reality were agencies meant to check and break down any resistance to the governmental policy (art. 17). Even the fact that the communal authorities still possessed the right to appoint the teachers had lost much of its meaning, since their choice was thenceforward restricted to graduates of the State-administered training-schools (art. 7). To complete the circle of an all-embracing State-control, art. 16 gave to the central government even the right to determine the curriculum of all communal schools.[7]

---

[6] Not only the Catholics, but also many honest-thinking Liberals were well aware that this "religious stipulation" was only a mere hypocritical and theoretical concession, for in practice the work of the clergy would be made impossible in such "progressive schools." Typical of this thinking are the words of the independent Liberal newspaper *"Chronique,"* which addressed the Liberal government with the words: "Your stipulation is only a trick, something unworthy of a government with self-respect."—Quoted in Verhaegen, *De Schoolstrijd in Belgie,* p. 34.

[7] It was in application of this article that on July 20, 1880, the first compulsory official "Curriculum for the primary schools" was published by the government.

The first public opposition to this proposed law came from the Belgian bishops who immediately directed their forthcoming traditional Lenten Pastoral Letter to the fathers of families. In this Pastoral they pointed out the truly anti-religious nature of a law that inevitably, despite all hypocritical concessions, would bring the country to the official "school without God." At the end of their letter, which was read in all the churches of the country, the bishops, desiring to make the faithful realize the far-reaching consequences of this new law, ordered that thenceforward at all Masses on Sundays this prayer be recited by all: "From schools without God, and from teachers without faith, deliver us, o Lord."

This letter indeed became the starting point for an orderly but vigorous campaign by both clergy and lay people against the admission of the proposed new school law. Just as they did fifty years earlier, under the Dutch rule, so now the moderate Liberals joined forces with the Catholics, by signing petitions asking the two Houses of Parliament to drop the draft-proposal altogether.

But not even 317,000 signatures of the heads of families, reppresenting ninety per cent of the population, could impress the Liberal government and its parliamentary majority. The Chamber of Representatives passed the law on June 6, 1879, by 67 votes against 60, and one abstention. Twelve days later the Senate approved the law with 33 votes against 31, and one abstention.[8] On July 1, Leopold II (1865-1909) gave his royal assent to the new law. Thus disappeared the last ray of hope from the minds of those who up to then had expected that the King would never sanction a law that had not only been passed by such a slight parliamentary majority, but was also contrary to the wishes of most of the citizens. On July 10, when the text of the law appeared in the

---

[8] Never in history has the passing of a law put into more bold relief the tremendous responsibility of the individual voting citizen than did this Belgian school law of 1879. The one vote that was to be decisive in the approval of the law by the Senate was the vote of the Liberal Senator Boyaval who, on the eve of his death, was nevertheless transported by his friends from his sickbed to the floor of the Senate. Senator Boyaval himself had been elected at Bruges with a winning margin of exactly one vote. It was therefore through the vote of one single citizen that the "Law of Misfortune" was made possible in the history of Belgium and of the Church.

official publication of the government, the *Moniteur,* the black band of mourning around the frontpage of the Catholic newspapers tolled the knell of political defeat for the Catholics; but the other pages were already vigorously outlining the plan for a tactical resistance by a Catholic nation to a law that already was a "law of ill omen."[9]

Petitions, protest-meetings and demonstrations, yea, even the official statements by the hierarchy, had proved themselves to be insufficient to stop the masonic drive for an atheistic elementary school system. The only way to keep Catholic children out of anti-Catholic schools was to provide the country with all the necessary Catholic institutions, so as to have in each locality a Catholic "school with God" next to the official "school without God"; for, despite this new law, Catholic citizens still had their constitutional freedom of instruction.

This was a logical and very simple solution in theory, but a tremendous and irksome task in practice. Less than three months were left to find the necessary teachers, buildings, and funds, to carry out this program, as the new school year would open at the end of September. But, no other way was really left open for the Catholics to enter into competition with a government which had power to dispose not only of the money of the taxpayers, but also of the buildings of the once Catholic schools that through the law of 1842 had become civil public schools.

As was to be expected, the bishops vigorously backed up the faithful in their plans for the erection of an independent Catholic school system. The guiding principles for the Catholics in their historical "School Fight" from 1879 till 1884 were to be found in the "Practical instructions for the use of confessors," promulgated on September 1, 1879.[10]

In most outspoken terms the bishops declared that in the particular circumstances of the Belgium of 1879 the civil public school had become a definite, proximate, and universal danger to faith and morals. Consequently all Catholics were forbidden to attend,

---

[9] Cf. Verhaegen, *op. cit.,* p. 52.

[10] The official text of these episcopal documents can be found in *La Belgique et le Vatican* (3 vols., Bruxelles: Bruylant-Christophe & Cie, 1880-1181).

to establish, or to administer such schools, or in any other direct or indirect way to co-operate in the new school law. From this general condemnation of the civil public school system the Practical Instructions deduced the duties of priests, parents, teachers, and school inspectors in particular.

Priests were not to provide the religious instruction in the school buildings placed at their disposal by the law. They were to use the pulpit, pastoral visitations, and personal conversations, to prevent the faithful from any participation in the civil public school system. At the same time, however, they were to avoid even the slightest insulting word against the teachers of such public schools and against the government officials, who especially were not to be referred to in the pulpit. It was furthermore proclaimed a most serious duty for all pastors to do their utmost to establish a Catholic school in their parish.

Parents sending their children to a civil public school were to be deemed guilty of grave sin. The only exception to this rule was the case wherein a serious reason justified such conduct of the parents, and wherein at the same time circumstances changed what was a proximate danger to faith and morals into a remote one.

Only for very exceptional reasons could a Catholic be permitted to continue teaching in the civil public schools. Such could be the case for a young man whose uninterrupted teaching profession was necessary for his definite exemption from military service. Such also for the elderly teacher who very soon would be entitled to his superannuation. Such likewise for the teacher who really could not resign without bringing himself or his family to a state of poverty. But, these exceptions were all to be brought to the notice of the local pastor who had to refer them to the bishop for the final judgment on the matter. The bishop, however, would grant such a dispensation only when a prudent presumption existed that in a particular school the school law *de facto* would not be applied, especially the part relating to the course in "common morality." Furthermore, the teacher receiving such a dispensation had to promise to resign immediately when it would no longer be possible to comply with these ecclesiastical instructions; he was not in any way to try to attract the children to his school if there was a Catholic school in the locality, nor was he himself to attempt to teach the catechism text independently or against the ecclesiastical authorities.

No dispensation of any kind would ever be granted to permit a Catholic to be an inspector of public instruction, for the reason simply that such officials were bound precisely to see to the application of the condemned law itself.

Catholics who persisted in a conduct contrary to these rules were to be deprived of sacramental absolution.

A stronger ecclesiastical condemnation of a civil law could hardly be imagined. Never before in Belgium's history had such an open break between Church and State existed. Were the Belgian bishops of 1879 right in so violently mobilizing all Catholic forces against the government, or would not a slightly mitigated protest have been more appropriate?

A few Catholic members of Parliament in those days, and particularly the future political leader of the Catholics, Charles Woeste (1837-1922), would have preferred a less rigid attitude on the part of the hierarchy.[11] The writer's judgment regarding the Belgian hierarchy in this matter is however that of Verhaegen who expressed the traditional feelings of practically all Catholics when he wrote: "The Belgian Catholics will never be sufficiently grateful to their bishops [of 1879] for having realized their duties so clearly, and for having fulfilled them with such courage and efficacy."[12]

It makes no sense, indeed, to question the right of the hierarchy to fight against a law hypocritically said to be legally passed by the constituted authorities. It has already been pointed out how this law was forced upon the nation by a slender parliamentary majority, which in no way reflected the mind of the majority of the people. But, even if such a law had been passed unanimously or with an overwhelming majority, it would still have been the duty and the right of the Belgian bishops of 1879 to lead their

---

[11] Cf. Woeste, *Mémoires pour servir à l'Histoire contemporaine de la Belgique* (3 vols., Bruxelles: A. Dewit, 1927-1937), I, p. 166.

[12] ". . . nooit zullen de Belgische Katholieken erkentelijk genoeg zijn aan hunne bisschoppen, om hunne verplichtingen met dusdanige helderheid ingezien en ze met zulke moedige krachtdadigheid vervuld te hebben."—*De Schoolstrijd in Belgie,* p. 59.

flock in the footsteps of the first bishop who, eighteen centuries earlier, had told the governments of all ages that we must always "obey God rather than men."[13]

It might be true that in other countries, with several religious denominations, a law like the Belgian school law of 1879 could be considered a step forward to an equitable solution of the so-called school problem. The text of this law, in the hands of a trustworthy government, could indeed lead to a more or less compromise situation acceptable to the parents, the Church and the State.[14] In the hands of the anti-Catholic Belgian government of 1879, however, this law was far from being a step to better understanding and mutual appreciation among citizens of a Catholic country. The hierarchy therefore was absolutely right in condemning the new school law from the very first moment, as being a systematic attack of Freemasonry against religion in general and against the Catholic Church in particular.

For, if the so-called "Catholic-confessional" law of 1842 had brought the Catholic school system to the verge of ruin notwithstanding successive Catholic parliamentary majorities, what good then could be expected from the Freemason-inspired irreligious law of 1879 to be put into effect by an anti-Catholic government?

The superficial concessions through which religious instruction was reputedly given some place in the public school system could not hoodwink the bishops. The late Cardinal Sterckx's naive confidence in the political honesty of the Liberals belonged definitely to the past, and his mistakes in the field of Catholic education were not to be repeated. This time the bishops let the whole country know that under the new law all civil public schools were meant to become institutions aimed at the gradual dechristianization of an overwhelmingly Catholic population. Only such a strong ecclesiastical condemnation could prevent the tactical strategy of the Liberals from succeeding, the more so when this strategy was all set to use any milder episcopal statement as a proof that Catholics should not completely disown the civil public school system. The

---

[13] Acts of the Apostles, V, 29.

[14] Cf. Burns, *The Catholic School System in the United States* (New York: Benziger Br., 1908), and *The Growth and Development of the Catholic School System in the United States* (New York: Benziger Br., 1912).

four following years of bitter fighting were to prove how rightly the bishops had judged the intentions and the tactics of the Freemason-led Liberals.[15]

The principles having thus been laid down by the bishops, the Catholic clergy and lay people immediately took up the tremendous task of organizing their own Catholic school system against a hostile government. In practice this meant that they had to build as many schools as necessary to keep Catholic children out of anti-Catholic schools; to secure the necessary funds for the support of these schools; and then to staff them with the proper teachers.

The general framework of the independent Catholic school system was to be in the hands of *School Committees* and *School Inspectors.*

Over the entire country the Catholic school committees were organized on local, district, and provincial levels. The *Local School Committee,* composed of five to ten fathers of families selected by the pastor, was the soul of the whole educational system. With the pastor as a permanent "member *de iure,*" the committee elected its own president, treasurer and secretary. The local committee was to use all possible means, such as visits to the homes and the distribution of books and pamphlets, to reveal the true school policy of the government and consequently to make Catholic parents conscious of their grave obligation to send their children to a Catholic school. The committee would collect, within its own parish, the funds necessary for the building and maintenance of its schools, and also nominate the teachers to be proposed by the inspector to the bishop for his final approval.

Immediately above the local committees came the *District Committee.* The dean of the district selected its members from the different local committees. Their main duty was to make a general survey of the educational conditions in the different localities, and to be the intermediary between the local and the provincial committees.

The *Provincial Committee,* composed of twenty to thirty outstanding members of the province, in great majority lay people,

---

[15] Cf. Verhaegen, *op. cit.,* p. 58.

was to meet at fixed times in the capital of the province. Besides a permanent body of directors the provincial committees had also different departments corresponding to the different needs of a modern school system. They were also to build up a pool of resources from which funds could be distributed to the most needy schools in the province. Finally, the provincial committees had also the care of the diocesan training schools for teachers.

Provisional and district *inspectors,* all lay specialists, were to supervise the technical side of these schools, while ecclesiastical inspectors were to see to the religious and moral education of the pupils.

The generosity of Belgium's Catholics from all classes of society provided the necessary financial means, while sometimes with true heroism teachers left their relatively well paid positions in civil public schools to form the teaching body of the new Catholic schools.[16]

The Liberals who in the beginning had jokingly despised the "paper anathemas" of the bishops became somewhat disconcerted when three months later three quarters of the local communities in the nation opened the new school year with an independent Catholic school. The first anniversary of the Law of Misfortune was certainly no occasion for excessive rejoicing among the Liberals either, when statistics revealed that in just one year the Belgian Catholics had established 2,064 schools, attended by more than three fifths of the country's elementary school population. Thus were verified the words of a Catholic member of Parliament who had told the Liberals during the discussion of the new law: "Something will be missing in your schools: the thing that will fill ours: the confidence of the families."[17]

---

[16] Cf. Verhaegen, *op. cit.,* pp. 65-90.

[17] Kervyn de Lettenhove: "Une seule chose manquera à vos écoles, et c'est ce qui remplira les nôtres; la confiance des familles."—*Annales parlementaires, Chambre des représentants,* session législative ordinaire de 1878-1879, p. 846.

Cf. *Rapport sur la Situation de l'Instruction primaire en Belgique, 1843-1896* (15 vols., Bruxelles: Ministère de l'Intérieur et de l'Instruction publique, 1846-1896); *Statistique des Écoles primaires, officielles et privées, au 31 décembre 1881* (Bruxelles: Chambre des Représentants-Commission d'Énquête scolaire, 1883).

The Liberal government now resorted to all means, including pressure of the lowest type and dictatorial threats, in order to stop the Catholics from further compliance with the directives of their bishops.[18] When these methods failed, the government tried to attack the episcopal authority in a direct way that certainly would have been effective if the Liberal plans had succeeded. The government namely used all the powers of secret diplomacy to bring the Vatican to a public disapproval of the rigid attitude of the Belgian hierarchy in the School Fight. When Pope Leo XIII, former nuncio at Brussels, refused to play the Liberal card, the Belgian government broke off its diplomatic relations with the Holy See on June 5, 1880.[19]

More than ever before the Liberal government was now determined to carry out the orders of the Freemason Lodges. Making use of taxes contributed among others by the Catholic citizens the government went on erecting the most extravagant school buildings in all local communities, disregarding the fact that very often the only pupils attending them would be the children of the teachers.[20] There is no need of saying that such an "immense political folly," as it was once called, brought with it a tremendous increase in taxes, since the government was running the country at the rate of an annual deficit of almost ten million francs. The School Fight, originally a straightout issue on moral and religious principles, now also became a matter of economical policy which was to increase, if possible, the unpopularity of the government.

Liberals could no longer deny the overwhelming Catholic victory in the School Fight when in 1884 statistics revealed that in five years of uneven struggle with the government the Belgian

---

[18] Cf. *Enquête scolaire* (5 vols., Bruxelles: Chambre des Représentants-Commission d'Enquête scolaire, 1881-1883); Verhaegen, *op. cit.*, pp. 133-150, and pp. 162-205 concerning the famous "school inquiry."

[19] Cf. *La Belgique et le Vatican* (3 vols., Bruxelles: Bruylant-Christophe & Cie, 1880-1881).

[20] A typical example of this situation was found in the province of Limburg where between 1878 and 1884 the number of civil public schools increased from 239 to 354 while the number of pupils attending them dropped from 24,635 to 5,187! !—Cf. Van Kalken, *La Belgique contemporaine*, p. 123, and *Histoire de Belgique*, pp. 553-554.

Catholics established 3,385 schools where 8,713 teachers provided for the education of the great majority of the population. The writing was definitely on the wall for the Masonic government of Belgium when a year before the elections of 1884 even some Liberals began to refer in their press to their own former "great Liberal government" as the "government of the uncapables, . . . a government that will remain notorious in Belgium's history as the most unworthy government since 1830, . . . a government that will be thrown into the grave, disdained and despised by the overwhelming majority of Belgium's citizens."[21]

A year later this Liberal prophecy became reality when the elections of June 10, 1884, brought the Catholics a majority of 34 in the Chamber of Representatives. The newspapers called this electoral result not so much a Liberal defeat as a Liberal crushing. In the capital itself, where Catholics and moderate Liberals, as they had done sixty years earlier, joined forces in the Independent Party, the outstanding defeated candidate was Minister Van Humbeeck himself whose family home—o irony of history!—through successive sales had already been transformed into a Catholic school! All over the country, in churches and public squares, an exultant *Te Deum* rose up from the lips of the Catholics.[22]

---

[21] Thus *Le National* on June 9, 1883, as quoted by Verhaegen, *De Schoolstrijd in Belgie,* pp. 212-213.

[22] Thus Verhaegen, *op. cit.,* p. 87 and p. 216.

CHAPTER VII

The Restoration Laws of 1884 and 1895

Historians may discuss whether the unexpectedly large Catholic victory in the elections of 1884 was due in the main to the anti-religious attitude of the government or rather to a sober reaction against the financial policy of the Liberals.[1] But, it can not be denied that the first measures taken by the new government were directly in agreement with the wishes of the Catholic majority of the people. Public instruction was brought again under the control of the Ministry of the Interior, and the Law of Misfortune was formally repealed when on July 23, 1884, a new school law was proposed. Before this law was passed on September 10th of the same year Parliament had already, on August 4th, approved the necessary appropriations for the resumption of diplomatic relations with the Holy See.

This third school law in Belgium's history, officially promulgated on September 20, 1884, had as its object the undoing of the Law of Misfortune and of the effects that resulted from the five years of the School Fight. The position of communal authorities in the educational field was strengthened as never before, while the central government ceased to have any direct rôle in the matter. The communes regained their right to organize their own schools or, with the consent of the provincial authorities, to recognize and make use of one or more existing private or denominational institutions. In practice this meant that the communal authorities themselves would determine the number and qualifications of schools and teachers needed in their territory, draw up the school curriculum and regulations, fix their budget, and appoint and pay the teachers. It was also left to the communal authorities to decide whether or not religious and moral instruc-

---

[1] Cf. Pirenne, *Histoire de Belgique,* VII, pp. 297-298, who left no doubt as to his opinion when he wrote: "Ce ne sont pas les principes, ce sont les intérêts qui ont décidé du résultat de l'élection."

tion would be part of the curriculum in their public schools. But in case they decided against such instruction, the central government could then force them to recognize and subsidize one or more denominational schools if at least twenty fathers of families requested it. On the other hand a similar request could be made which would guarantee the establishment of an a-religious school in a commune where parents demanded it.

If everyone had only accepted the supreme right of the father to determine the philosophical orientation of the education of his children, this new law would have given satisfaction to all citizens and thus would have happily ended a school controversy that had far too long divided the nation.

But no; a law based upon respect for all religious and philosophical opinions was no longer acceptable to the leading lights of the Grand Orient. A government whose sole purpose was to remedy the unjust measures of the Law of Misfortune was dubbed by the Liberals a bunch of reactionary characters of the old regime.[2] Thus a law which had intended to put an end to the School Fight merely served the purpose of rekindling the old bitter feud that was to last for the thirty years the Catholic government was to remain in power.

Street riots and Liberal electoral victories on the local level were used by King Leopold II to justify his legally questionable intervention that forced the Catholic cabinet of Malou-Jacobs-Woeste to resign.[3] Successive governments, however, were still to owe their position to the Catholic majority whose principles would always be the same despite tactical switches from "hard" to "soft" personalities to whom would be entrusted the duty of carrying out the government's program.[4]

---

[2] Cf. Pirenne, *op. cit.*, VII, p. 300; Van Kalken, *La Belgique contemporaine*, pp. 125-126.

[3] Cf. de Lichtervelde, *La Monarchie en Belgique sous Léopold Ier et Léopold II* (Bruxelles et Paris: Librairie nationale d'art et d'histoire, 1921), pp. 57-58.

[4] Cf. van der Smissen, *Léopold II et Beernaert. d'après leur correspondance inédite* (2 vols., Bruxelles: A. Goemaere, 1920); also Carton de Wiart, *Beernaert et son Temps* (Bruxelles: Renaissance du Livre, 1945); Woeste, *Échos des Luttes contemporaines, 1895-1905* (Bruxelles: Schepens & Cie, 1906).

Following the same trend the fourth Belgian school law, the law of September 15, 1895, complemented the law of 1884. In two important points the autonomy of the local communes, as sanctioned in 1884, was restricted. First of all, to prevent local authorities from abusing the law of 1884 against the wishes of the population, the communes had no longer the right to decide whether religious instruction would or would not be included in the curriculum of their schools. Religious instruction was thenceforth to be compulsory again in all civil public schools.

At first sight this specification has the appearance of being another "Catholic victory," but in fact it was not so. In practice this point of the law was only confirming the actual situation in most communes where the local authorities had made religion part of the curriculum since 1884.[5] The real "step forward" of this new law is to be found in its additional specification ordering that thenceforth compulsory religious instruction should be given either at the beginning or at the end of the class hours.

The only purpose of this specification was to meet the greater convenience of those pupils who, at the request of their parents, were dispensed from attending the religious course. The government's desire to respect all philosophical convictions was even made more clear by the official interpretation of the law as given by Minister Schollaert who explained that the general teaching in a civil public school class had to be absolutely a-confessional even if only one pupil was legally dispensed from the formal course in religion.[6]

---

[5] Thus was the situation in 4,042 out of 4,195 communal public schools, as reported by the Minister of Public Instruction, Poullet, to Parliament on December 18, 1913.—*Annales parlementaires, Chambre des Représentants,* session législative ordinaire de 1913-1914, p. 387. Cf. also *Situation de l'Enseignement primaire et des Oeuvres scolaires d'Ordre social* (Bruxelles: Ministère de l'Intérieur et de l'Instruction publique, Administration centrale de l'Enseignement primaire, 1903).

[6] "N'y eût-il qu'un seul enfant dispensé du cours de religion, l'instituteur sera tenu de s'abstenir, dans son enseignement scientifique, de toute considération se rapportant aux dogmes de la religion; non seulement il devra, conformément aux prescriptions de l'article 6 de la loi organique, s'abstenir de toute attaque contre les convictions religieuses des familles dont les enfants lui sont confiés, mais som enseignement ne pourra être impregné d'aucun

Although non-Catholic historians still continue to refer to the government of 1895 as the "openly clerical cabinet de Burlet-Schollaert," the educational policy of this government proves more than anything else that Catholic political leaders had taken to heart the warning the King already gave them in 1884 when he wrote to Premier Malou: "After 1878 the Liberals acted as if there were no longer Catholics in Belgium; it behooves Catholics now not to forget that there is a great number of Liberals in the country."[7]

Catholics, who in the main were far from enthusiastic over this concession which weakened the confessional character of the civil public school, were more pleased with the other restriction placed on local autonomy by the new law. Overruling those anti-Catholic communal authorities who systematically continued to refuse any financial aid to Catholic schools, the central government was thenceforward directly to subsidize such schools and equally to divide its subsidies between the civil public schools and all confessional schools willing to adopt both an official curriculum and a State inspection.[8]

Liberals, forgetting their own historical background, protested vigorously against what they called a scandalous and partisan attack on local autonomy of the communes. In all their anti-Catholic moves Liberals thenceforward could rely on the support of

---

principe confessionel; en d'autres termes, il n'entretiendra ses élèves ni des dogmes, ni de ce qui différencie un culte d'un autre."—Ministerial circular of October 1, 1895, in *Bulletin du Ministère de l'Instruction publique,* XII (1895), p. 147.

[7] "Après 1878 les libéraux ont agi comme s'il n'y avait plus de catholiques en Belgique. L'intérêt des catholiques maintenant est de ne pas oublier qu'il y a dans le pays un très grand nombre de libéraux."—Quoted by Van Kalken, *La Belgique contemporaine,* p. 126.

[8] Besides these two principal restrictions the new law also imposed minor restrictions of a technical nature. To suppress a school or a class communes needed thenceforth the approval of the higher authorities, and thus the teaching profession acquired a guarantee of relative permanency. Teaching salaries were stabilized in accordance with fixed standards. To remedy too arbitrary appointments by certain communes the new law also provided that only after at least five years of teaching could one apply for nomination as school principal.

the Socialists who as an organized party had entered the political field in 1885 and the Belgian Parliament in 1894.[9]

The Catholic government meanwhile marched on unimpressed by "spontaneous" street demonstrations, strong in its conviction that it had the support of the nation in recalling to the local authorities the primary and supreme educational rights of the fathers of families.[10] The fact that the elections of 1898 even reenforced the Catholic majority in Parliament strengthened this conviction of the government but did not end the school controversy. More than ever before, anti-Catholic provincial and communal authorities, with a strange conception of their real rôle in the nation, kept boycotting the central government by discriminatingly excluding denominational schools from all provincial and communal aid and by eliminating completely the religious spirit from their own schools.[11]

When in February, 1910, no less than nine sessions of the Chamber of Representatives were devoted to the discussion of the school policy of the Catholic government, it became evident that the gap between Catholics and non-Catholics was wider than ever before.

In the past the Liberals had rather been fighting the Catholic-confessional character of the civil public school, but had always, at least in theory, reserved some place for the common religious and moral principles in the general education of the civil public school system. Even in the heated moments of the School Fight, between 1879 and 1884, many Liberals, more anti-clerical than anti-religious, still believed in the principle that there could be no

---

[9] Cf. Bertrand, *Histoire de la Démocratie et du Socialisme en Belgique depuis 1830* (2 vols., Bruxelles: Dechesne & Cie, 1905-1907); Destrée-Vandervelde, *Le Socialisme en Belgique* (Paris: Bibliothèque socialiste internationale, 1903); Garsou, *L'Évolution du Parti libéral à Bruxelles, 1841-1939* (Bruxelles: Imprimerie du Marais, 1939); Vandervelde, *Le Parti ouvrier belge de 1885 à 1925* (Bruxelles: L'Églantine, 1925).

[10] How difficult it is for the Liberal mind to understand and appreciate this Catholic "family policy" becomes evident when it is considered that a genuine historian like Van Kalken continues to refer to this period of Belgian history as one of sectarian oppression by the Catholic government. Cf. his *La Belgique contemporaine*, p. 155.

[11] Cf. Van Kalken, *Histoire de Belgique*, pp. 561-562.

education without some religious orientation. To them the civil public school, regardless of the wishes of parents, should not be Catholic, nor Protestant, nor Jewish, but still should definitely have its spiritual values and provide for its pupils a "common morality" based on belief in God and the immortality of the soul.

Liberals and Socialists of 1910, however, were fighting openly for that civil public "school without God" that the Belgian bishops already in 1879 had prophetically revealed as the inevitable consequence of the Liberal "progressive school."[12]

Catholics, on their side, were now relatively well organized, with the result that bishops and priests could devote themselves exclusively to their proper spiritual and cultural task, leading the leadership of their flock in the social and political domains to trustworthy and capable laymen.[13]

On March 14, 1911, Minister Frans Schollaert (1851-1917) introduced a parliamentary bill that tended to make a legal reality of the resolution adopted in the Catholic Congress of 1909, by which Catholics claimed full equality for all schools in the matter of subsidies from the State, the provinces, and the communes. This new draft-proposal called for many important reforms as, for example, free and compulsory instruction for all children under fourteen years of age. But, its typical point was the introduction of the so-called "school coupon." Each year the government was to give to a father who had children of school age a coupon which was to be handed to the controlling authorities of the school of his choice. This coupon would entitle these authorities to a proportionate subsidy from the commune, the province, and the central government, in the ratio of three-tenths, one-tenth and six-tenths of the school expenses. The value of these coupons was to be such that fifty of them would enable the school authorities to pay the salary of one teacher and to provide one class with the

---

[12] Cf. *Annales parlementaires, Chambre des représentants,* session législative ordinaire de 1910-1911, particularly the session of July 17, 1911, pp. 1921-1966.

[13] Cf. Defourny, *Les Congrès catholiques en Belgique* (Louvain, 1908); Moyersoen, *Prosper Poullet en de Politiek van zijn Tijd* (Brugge: Desclée-De Brouwer, 1946).

necessary furniture and equipment. The construction of the school buildings and their maintenance would still be left entirely to the respective civil, private, or ecclesiastical authorities, while the general inspection of these schools would be in the hands of the civil authority alone.

It really is difficult to imagine a school law that would safeguard more perfectly and co-ordinate more harmoniously the rights of the family, the Church, and the State. No wonder that Catholics all over the country started an enthusiastic campaign for the passing of this proposed law.[14] Anti-Catholic Liberals and Socialists on their side joined forces in the first official appearance of the Leftist-cartel which was more successful in its policy of parliamentary obstruction than in that of engendering a spirit of opposition among the people to a proposed law which once and forever could bring about the real solution of the school problem.[15]

The Catholic parliamentary majority was ready to pass the proposed law despite the temporary obstructionist maneuvers of a fanatical minority, and the nation would have seen the long expected equitable and just ending of the unfortunate and unnecessary school controversy. But, the totally unexpected and incomprehensible personal intervention of King Albert (1875-1934), backed by the even more questionable attitude of the only dissenting Catholic deputy, Charles Woeste, forced the Catholic cabinet to resign.[16] Never again would a similar opportunity to end the school controversy present itself.

---

[14] The text of the draft-proposal was drawn up in the form of a question-answer pamphlet by the future Minister Van Overbergh, at that time Secretary-General to the Minister of Arts and Sciences who was the responsible authority in the field of public instruction. Under the title *"Le Projet de Loi scolaire. Ce que tout Père de Famille doit savoir"* 2,500,000 copies of it were distributed by the *Comité national de Propagande.*

[15] Representatives of the new Socialist party entered the Belgian Parliament when the first "plural suffrage" elections of 1894 sent 34 Socialists to the Chamber of Representatives, leaving only 14 seats to the Liberals, but with 104 Catholics still possessing a strong majority.

[16] Cf. *Annales parlementaires. Chambre des Représentants,* session législative ordinaire de 1910-1911, pp. 1446-1450, 1455-1456.

Later history will pass judgment on those responsible for this.[17] But the tremendous demonstration immediately organized by the Belgian Catholics to honor the resigned Minister Schollaert, the father of the school coupon idea, left no doubt about the feelings of the people of those days for the ones who were responsible for having prevented the end of the school controversy. Nine months later the feelings of the same people were even more clearly manifested when with the elections of June 2, 1912, the Catholic parliamentary majority increased to eighteen.[18] Of course, there is no doubt that this Catholic victory was in great part due to the successful governing strategy of true Catholic statesmen for a period of more than a quarter of a century.[19] But, it was definitely also a personal victory for Premier Charles de Broqueville (1860-1940) and his Minister in charge of Public Instruction, Prosper Poullet (1868-1937).[20]

---

[17] The Catholic historian from Louvain-University, van der Essen, calls the idea of the school coupon an "equitable solution of the school problem."—(*Deux mille ans d'Histoire,* p. 121.) Meanwhile his Liberal colleague from the Brussels-University, Van Kalken, calls it a "despicable project," and praises King Albert for having prevented the "adventurous enterprise" of the Catholic government.—(*Histoire de Belgique,* pp. 563-564).

[18] Before this date the Catholic majority had been steadily on the downgrade. From 26 in 1902 it dropped to 20 in 1904, to 12 in 1906, to 8 in 1908, and to 6 in 1910.

[19] Cf. de Henricourt de Grunne, *Vingt-cinq Années de Gouvernement* (Bruxelles: A. Dewit, 1910), particularly chapter III concerning public instruction, pp. 130-188. Compare with Hymans, *Histoire parlementaire de Belgique, 1830-1910* (9 vols., Bruxelles: Bruylant-Christophe, 1878-1910).

[20] Since May 2, 1907, the Department of Education had officially been named the Ministry of Sciences and Arts. By royal decree of December 17, 1932, the name was changed to the Ministry of Public Instruction.

CHAPTER VIII

The Reconciliation Law of 1919 and Its Present-Day Application

Over and above urgent decisions regarding the military policy of the country there was still the unsolved school problem that called for the special attention of the newly re-enforced government of 1912.[1] Mainly for reasons of political opportunism Poullet gave up the idea of the school coupon as proposed by his predecessor Schollaert. He presented instead his own draft-proposal which was the fruit of years of personal study and sincere seeking after an equitable solution.

Already before the last elections he had publicly in Parliament made his own the words of Cardinal Mercier (1851-1926) who, on April 14, 1909, had openly declared that Catholics did not fight or hope for the ultimate substitution of all civil public schools by confessional Catholic schools for all children in the nation.[2] The draft-law now proposed by Poullet was the official proof of his desire to reconcile two existing school systems in the country: the official civil public school, and the denominational confessional school, both of which had already become part and parcel of the nation's patrimony.

---

[1] Cf. Moyersoen, *Prosper Poullet en de Politiek van zijn Tijd,* pp. 119-154.

[2] ". . . nous ne voulons pas opposer l'école libre aux écoles officielles: ce serait à la fois une erreur et une folie. Grâce à Dieu, il existe de très bonnes écoles officielles. . . . Nos adversaires auront pour tactique de dire que nous sommes opposés à l'enseignement officiel. Prévenons cette imputation. Nous la désavouons par avance et la déclarons calomnieuse. La vérité est que nous déplorons qu'il faille des écoles libres. L'idéal serait que l'enseignement officiel fût en rapport avec les convictions et les droits de tous, et assez respectueux des consciences pour ne pas imposer aux catholiques les sacrifices que réclament d'eux la création et l'entretien d'un enseignement privé."—*Annales parlementaires, Chambre des Représentants,* session législative ordinaire de 1911-1912, pp. 2009-2010.

Introduced on June 20, 1913, the proposed law contained many important innovations. For the first time in Belgium instruction was to be made compulsory for all children. The pedagogical value of the primary school was to be improved through the institution of a "fourth grade" with a more professional orientation. Instruction was to be completely free as the provinces would be obliged to provide the necessary equipment for the children of all schools. Equality for all was furthermore to be guaranteed as communes and provinces had to make available to every child their "school services," such as food, clothing, recreational facilities, etc. Finally, the proposed law was to confirm more than ever the freedom of the fathers of families: Subsidies for confessional schools were to be increased, but at the same time the erection of a-confessional civil schools was to be made more easy. Whereas under the law of 1895 the request of twenty fathers was necessary, now, under the new law, the wishes of the heads of families representing twenty children of school age was to suffice for constraining the commune to erect such a civil public school.

During forty-eight sessions that lasted no less than four months, the Chamber of Representatives debated the new law. In the Senate also, the debates took from April 3, till May 14, 1914. With masterly self-restraint Minister Poullet defended his proposal, reassuring his opponents that the new law was not at all a hidden maneuver leading to the omnipotent dominion of the "congregational schools," as the Liberals and Socialists liked to call the Catholic schools with members of religious congregations on the teaching staff.[3]

With solid legal arguments he explained how subsidies to the confessional Catholic school system were in perfect accordance with both the letter and the spirit of the Constitution, especially since the new law would also proclaim the principle of free and compulsory instruction for all.[4]

His convincing logic also succeeded in quelling the outspoken anti-religious outbursts made at the last moment by some Liberals.

[3] Cf. *Annales parlementaires, Chambre des Représentants,* session législative ordinaire de 1912-1913, pp. 2629-2634.

[4] Cf. *Annales parlementaires, Chambre des Représentants,* session législative ordinaire de 1913-1914, pp. 206-209.

Thus Parliament rejected the amendment of Feron who wanted the "re-introduction of the law of 1884" that left it to the communal authorities to decide whether or not religious instruction would be part of the school curriculum. Poullet here reminded Feron of the essential part of the law of 1884 which had apparently escaped the memory of the Liberal deputy, namely that twenty fathers of families could force a commune to either make religion part of the curriculum in the civil public school or to adopt and subsidize an existing confessional school.

A similar fate befell the amendment of Van de Walle who wanted a special course of "lay morality" for children who were legally dispensed from the course in religion. In this regard Poullet pointed out that the new school law was merely to supply a sanction for the existing conditions which originated in the free choice of the fathers of families. Of their own accord the fathers of families had brought "religion" into 4,042 of the 4,195 existing civil public schools, while for only three per cent of the 900,000 school children had a dispensation from the religious course been requested.[5]

On February 18, 1914, the law was passed in the Chamber of Representatives with 98 of the 100 Catholics voting in favor of it. The Liberal-Socialist minority had left the floor, shouting "The school fight will go on! Down with this new school law!" At the same time Woeste expressed the feelings of the Catholics when he congratulated Poullet, the father of this fifth school law in Belgium's history, with the words: "The work that is being accomplished here, is a work of liberty, equality, and justice, and therefore a work of peace and tolerance. We are alone in passing this law, and we are proud of it before our conscience, before the public opinion, and before the country."[6] A similar demonstration took place in the Senate on May 14.

---

[5] Cf. *Annales parlementaires, Chambre des Représentants,* session législative ordinaire de 1913-1914, pp. 376-384, 387, 817-822.

[6] "L'oeuvre qui s'achève est, à nos yeux, une oeuvre de liberté, d'égalité et de justice. Je dis aussi et par là même qu'elle est une oeuvre de paix et de tolérance. Nous sommes seuls à voter la loi: nous nous en glorifions vis-à-vis de notre conscience, vis-à-vis de l'opinion publique et vis-à-vis du pays."—*Annales parlementaires, Chambre des Représentants,* session législative ordinaire de 1913-1914, p. 1078.

For the time being this fifth school law in Belgium's history, promulgated on May 19, 1914, could not be applied, as the first World-War was soon to upset the peaceful policy of the country. When on August 4, 1914, the armies of the Kaiser attacked their little neighbor on the west, Belgians forgot their differences, with only Cardinal Mercier's "patriotism and endurance" as their common guiding light.[7] A government of "national union," composed of Catholics, Liberals, and Socialists, became the genuine expression of the nation's common stand against aggression.

This "sacred union," sealed with the blood of 46,000 Belgians who lost their lives and of 50,000 who had been invalided, continued after the war when for the first time since 1842 Belgium reappeared among the family of nations as a strong united country. The old unfortunate school controversy was definitely a thing of the past when on October 13, 1919, Parliament, after merely one hour of deliberation, unanimously passed the law submitted by de Broqueville to confirm and to complete the once so debated school law of 1914.[8]

This law of 1919, the sixth school law in Belgium's history, is up to the present day the charter of the country's elementary school system. Subsequent laws, royal decrees, and ministerial circulars clarified the provisions of this basic law, but its essential conciliatory principles were left intact.[9]

---

[7] Cf. Mayence, *La Correspondance de S. E. le Cardinal Mercier avec le Gouvernement Général allemand pendant l'Occupation 1914-1918* (Bruxelles: Dewit, 1919); Gille-Ooms-Delandsheere, *Cinquante mois d'occupation allemande 1914-1918* (3 vols., Bruxelles: Dewit, 1919).

[8] Cf. *Annales parlementaires, Chambre des Représentants,* session législative ordinaire de 1919-1920, pp. 2087-2096, 2136-2137.

[9] Together with a commentary, the text of the law of 1919, and all its additional prescriptions which govern the present Belgian elementary school system, can be found in Bauwens, *Code de l'Enseignement primaire* (12. ed., Bruxelles: L'Édition universelle, 1949), and *Code de l'Enseignement primaire et de l'Enseignement normal primaire* (12. ed., supplément, Bruxelles: L'Édition universelle, 1951). Cf. also De Schepper-Vansiliette, *Wet tot Regeling van het Lager Onderwijs* (Lier: Van In, 1948); Troch, *Wet tot Regeling van het Lager Onderwijs en Model Reglement* (6. ed., Lier: Van In, 1951).

From the canonical viewpoint of particular interest are the specifications which directly or indirectly affect the educational rights of parents and the Church. Such are the specifications regarding compulsory school attendance, the status of various denominational schools, public funds for denominational schools, school aid to children, and the place reserved for religious instruction in the civil public school system.

A. COMPULSORY SCHOOL ATTENDANCE

Articles 1 and 3 of the basic law of May 19, 1914, lay down the general principle by stating that all heads of families must see to it that proper elementary instruction is given to their children between six and fourteen years of age. Article 2, concerning the suspension of this obligation, and article 12, protecting the freedom of the heads of families, claim more attention here than the articles dealing with the technical applications of this principle.[10]

---

[10] *Art. 1.*—Les chefs de famille sont tenus de faire donner ou de donner à leurs enfants une instruction primaire convenable conformément aux dispositions de la présente loi.

Ils s'acquittent de cette obligation:

1) En faisant instruire leurs enfants dans une école publique ou privée du degré primaire ou moyen;

2) En les faisant instruire à domicile.

Art. 2.—L'obligation imposée à l'article précédent est suspendue: . . .

2) Lorsque les parents ou tuteurs opposent des griefs de conscience à l'envoi de leurs enfants ou pupilles dans toute école située dans un rayon de quatre kilomètres de leur habitation;

Art. 3.—L'obligation s'étend sur une période de huit années. Cette période commence après les vacances d'été de l'année pendant laquelle l'enfant accomplit sa sixième année, et se termine après que l'enfant a consacré huit années aux études.

Art. 12.—Sera puni d'une amende de 50 à 500 francs quiconque, pour déterminer un chef de famille à placer son enfant dans une école ou à le retirer d'une école, aura usé à son égard de voies de fait, de violence ou de menaces, ou lui aura fait craindre de perdre son emploi ou d'exposer à un dommage sa personne, sa famille ou sa fortune.

Si le coupable est fonctionnaire, officier public ou chargé d'un service public, l'amende pourra être portée au double.

Il est interdit à toute école primaire ou gardienne soumise au régime de la

Among the recognized cases wherein the principle of compulsory school attendance is not to be applied, art. 2 cites the case wherein the parents or guardians conscientiously object to sending their children to any of the schools within four kilometers from their residence.

This provision seeks to eliminate any conflict between the application of a civil law and one's religious or philosophical convictions. In view of the number and the variety of schools in all parts of the country, this specification has become mainly theoretical. But, if it should ever happen that anyone sought recourse to this article of the law, it then becomes the duty of a school inspector to investigate the sincerity of the objection. If the inspector himself doubted the good faith of the objector, he should then refer the case to the Court for a final decision. But, let it be noted that it is not within the province of either the inspector or the judge to probe the reasons for this objection. Their task is merely to pass judgment on the sincerity of the person in question in order to distinguish between the one who conscientiously upholds religious convictions and the dodger who just wants to defy the law.[11]

Of far more practical value is art. 12, aimed not only at eliminating exaggerated competition between different school systems, but even more so at protecting the freedom and the educational rights of parents. "Whoever makes use of violence, or threatens a father of a family with the loss of employment or personal, family, or financial misfortune, in order to compel him to enroll his child in a particular school, is liable to a fine of between fifty and five hundred francs. If the guilty one be a public official the fine may be doubled." This law was complemented by the law of August 14, 1948, stating that "after the first month of the school year it is forbidden for any school which is subject to the pro-

---

loi d'accepter, sans motifs légitimes, après un délai d'un mois suivant le début de l'année scolaire, un élève venant d'une autre école.

Dans tous les cas, l'appréciation de ces motifs est laissée au ministre de l'instruction publique. *Loi du 14 août 1948.*

[11] In the few cases that were ever brought to Court, judges have rather given a wider interpretation of the term "conscientious objection," applying it even to cases where walking along certain roads to school was considered a physical or moral danger for some children.

visions of the law, to accept a pupil from another school, without reasonable excuse."

Anyone who realizes the educational setbacks that result from changing schools in the middle of the year will readily admit that such a law is justified. Besides, a legal stipulation of this kind can hardly be considered an encroachment on the parental authority. As explained in the Ministerial Circular No. P 143/M17 of November 20, 1948, and confirmed in practice, a sufficient reason for such a change of school would obtain when parents move from one locality to another too distant from the previous school. Any change of school is also permitted to the parents during the first month of the school year, for it is the mind of the legislator that this period should suffice for them to form an opinion concerning the institution to which they would entrust their children. If after the first month they should still wish for other reasons, to enroll their child in another school, it is then the right of the district inspector, and eventually of the Minister of Public Instruction, to judge the seriousness of the alleged reasons. These reasons could be, for example, complaints about the disciplinary or educational methods of a certain school. But, above all it must be made certain that such a sudden change of school is not the result of some unhealthy partisan propaganda against another school system, or even just a means of acquiring material profit.

Besides, the total safeguarding of the parental freedom becomes even more evident when one remembers that all these legal specifications affect only those schools which are administered or at least subsidized by the government, and in no way touch the non-subsidized private or denominational schools.

B. VARIOUS DENOMINATIONAL SCHOOLS

1. The Independent School

Abstracted from any and every particular school law, provision for freedom of instruction is always guaranteed by art. 17 of the Constitution.[12] No private citizen, nor any Church-body in Bel-

[12] Cf. Chapter IV of this study.

gium can therefore be prevented from establishing and organizing any school, private or denominational. The first article of the present school law merely confirms this constitutional freedom by stating that attendance at private schools is one of the ways of complying with the prescription of compulsory school attendance.

For such completely independent private or denominational institutions there is no State intervention of any kind. The State, not having any control over them, regards them most logically also as non-existent when there is question of permitting schools to issue official certificates of studies or of granting financial support to them.

2. The Adopted School

Very few denominational elementary schools in Belgium have a status of total independence. On the contrary, most denominational schools come under the regime of the law of 1919 and its later complements.

The fundamental principle of the whole elementary school system in Belgium is to be found in articles 1 and 3 of the law of June 10, 1937, which modified articles 13 and 14 of the basic school law of 1919.[13]

The principle is this: In each commune there must be at least one civil public elementary school, located in a suitable building and having all the equipment necessary for the carrying out of the curriculum. Such a school is usually referred to as the "communal school," the "official school," or the "public school"; it is usually established in a public communal building and immediately directed by the local civil authorities, who appoint the teachers,

---

[13] *Art. 1.*—Toute commune est tenue de créer et d'entretenir au moins une école primaire communale, établie dans un local convenable et pourvue d'un outillage didactique répondant aux exigences pédagogiques qu'impose l'exécution du programme. . . .

Art. 3.—Si la commune reste en défaut de satisfaire à ses obligations légales déterminées par les articles 1 et 2 ci-dessus dans le délai de six mois à partir de la première invitation du ministre de l'instruction publique, les dispositions nécessaires seront décrétées d'office par arrête royal délibéré en Conseil des ministres, qui désignera, après enquête sur place, un commissaire spécial chargé de l'exécution de ces mesures. . . .

draw up school regulations and curriculum, and take care of all expenses. Should local authorities refuse or neglect to set up a public elementary school in their territory, then the central government would peremptorily establish one at the expense of the commune. And to insure the education of all children, the law also requires communal schools to provide complete primary instruction, that is the four grades extended over eight years of study. For the same reason the law requires communal schools to be truly public, that is, open to all children of both sexes.

The chief exception to this general principle is found in article 7 of the same law of 1937 permitting under certain conditions the replacement of a communal civil public school with an "adopted" private or denominational institution.[14] Since most existing Catholic elementary schools in Belgium are such, a description in detail of this typical Belgian institution of the "adoption of schools" is here useful.[15]

a) The act of adoption.

The "adoption of a school" is a legal act by which a communal council grants certain privileges to a private or denominational school, which in turn agrees to submit to certain directions, in order to insure the proper instruction of the children of the locality.

This bilateral agreement is drawn up in the form of a contract signed by both the College of Burgomaster and Aldermen and the so-called "titulary" of the adoption. This titulary can be an individual, such as the owner, the director, or the principal of the school; it can also be a "school-committee." In the latter case the members of such a committee have to be designated *nominatim* in

[14] *Art. 7.*—La commune peut adopter une ou plusieurs écoles privées.

L'adoption peut être consentie pour une durée de six ans au plus. Elle prendra fin avant cette date en cas de décès ou de retraite du titulaire sous le nom duquel l'adoption a été consentie. Elle peut toujours être renouvelée, même avant l'échéance.

Lorsque aucune convention n'a fixé la durée de l'adoption, la suppression de l'adoption ne peut être prononcée dans le courant d'une année scolaire, ni sans un préavis d'une année.

[15] The technical words used in the official documents are: adoption des écoles, aanneming van scholen; école adoptée, aangenomen school.

the contract, since a bilateral convention always presupposes a personal acceptation of rights and duties. In the case of most adopted Catholic schools the school contract is signed for the school by a committee of which the members are: the local pastor as honorary president, usually an assistant pastor as secretary, the principal of the school, and at least two lay men who respectively act as president and treasurer.

The adoption of a school falls under the exclusive domain of the local civil authorities who can adopt as many schools in their territory as they want, provided the financial status of the commune is sound and all the conditions required by the law are fulfilled. No approval by any higher authority is therefore needed.

It is true that the deliberations of the communal council preceding the adoption of a certain school, as well as the resulting contract, must be sent to the Governor of the province and to the Minister of Public Instruction. But, the law exclusively imposes this in order to permit these higher authorities to make sure that all legal specifications have been carried out.

The only legal limitation to this local autonomy exists when the communal authority goes so far in its policy of adopting private and denominational schools as to replace even the generally required civil public school with such an adopted institution. To do this there is required a special intervention of the King, who only after consulting with the Permanent Deputies of the province can grant such an authorization.[16] Besides, such a complete replacement of the civil public schools with adopted institutions can not even be authorized by the King, if in a community there are twenty children of school age whose parents petition for the establishment or the retention of a civil public school in the locality.[17]

---

[16] For the internal organization of communal, provincial, and central government in Belgium, cf. this study, pp. 62-63.

[17] To make sure, however, that such a petition originates as the free request of the parents, without any pressure, art. 8 of the law of June 10, 1937, states analogously with art. 12 of the basic school law: "Sera puni d'une amende de 50 à 500 francs, quiconque, pour déterminer un chef de famille à faire usage du droit de réclamer l'enseignement dans une école communale, à s'abstenir d'en faire usage, à signer une demande ou à la retirer, aura

b) The conditions of adoption.

To make sure that only deserving institutions could ever become the beneficiaries of this legal adoption, art. 15 of the basic school law of 1919 specifies the various conditions, all of which are essential conditions for any financial support from either the State, the province, or the commune. These conditions affect the school building, the qualifications of the teachers, the curriculum, the inspection, and the free character of the school attendance.[18]

The school has to be in what the law calls "a suitable building." This refers to the general location of the school, the size of the classrooms in relation to the number of the pupils, the ventilation and heating of the classrooms, etc.

The teachers must be Belgian citizens either by birth or by naturalization, and possess one of the official diplomas required for teachers in civil public schools.[19] It is worthy of note, however, that such official teacher diplomas can be obtained not only after studies in an official governmental "normal school," but

---

usé à son égard de voies de fait, de violences ou de menaces, ou lui aura fait craindre de perdre son emploi ou d'exposer à un dommage sa personne, sa famille ou sa fortune.—Si le coupable est fonctionnaire, officier public, ou chargé d'un service public, l'amende pourra être portée au double."

[18] *Art. 15.*—Aucune école primaire privée ne peut être adoptée à moins de se soumettre aux conditions suivantes:

1) L'école doit être établie dans un local convenable;

2) Sous réserve des situations acquises au 1er janvier 1914, les membres du personnel enseignant devront être Belges.

Ils devront être diplômés ou avoir subi l'examen dont il est fait mention à l'article 24.

3) Si l'enseignement de la religion fait partie du programme, cet enseignement sera donné au commencement ou à la fin des heures de classe. Les enfants dont les parents en font la demande seront dispensés d'y assister.

4) Le programme d'enseignement comprendra les matières énumérées à l'article 17.

5) L'école adoptée doit être soumise au régime de l'inspection de l'État établi en vertu de la présente loi.

6) . . . Aucune école primaire privée ne pourra être subventionnée par l'État, par la province ou par la commune, si elle ne réunit les conditions requises pour l'adoption par le présent article. . . .

[19] An exception to this rule was justly made in favor of those who were duly appointed teachers before January 1, 1914.

also through equivalent studies in provincial, communal, denominational, or private training schools that have been recognized by the central government.[20]

The curriculum of these schools must include all the subjects that are obligatory in civil public schools, and especially the required religious and moral instruction.[21] Since most schools applying for legal adoption are confessional schools, such a specification does not present any difficulty at all. But, on the other hand, legal adoption does not weaken the confessional character of the school. Those who have charge of an adopted denominational school are therefore not in any way obliged to admit pupils of other denominations. Only when an adopted confessional school is actually the only public school in the locality, then the children of all denominations must be admitted. In such a case the school takes on the character of a communal civil public school, and as such is subject to the special "religious provisions" which will later receive their due explanation in this study.

Legal adoption automatically brings with it on the part of the central government the inspection of all branches except the course of religion and morality, which remains under the exclusive control of the ecclesiastical authorities.[22]

Apart from this State inspection of the technical side of education, the authorities of adopted schools retain intact all their unfettered rights of directing and supervising their own institutions. This is particularly true for the appointment of teachers, and of medical inspectors, whose names are sent to the civil authorities for a *pro forma* approval.

Does all this mean that, despite this legal adoption by the communal council, the local civil government does not acquire any direct authority over such adopted schools? It means exactly that.

---

[20] *Art. 24.*—Les instituteurs communaux sont choisis parmi les Belges par la naissance ou la naturalisation, porteurs de diplômes d'instituteur primaire, sortis d'une école normale publique ou inspectée, . . .

[21] *Art. 17.*—L'instruction primaire comprend nécessairement l'enseignement de la religion et de la morale, . . .

[22] *Art. 39.*—L'inspection des écoles communales, des écoles adoptées et des écoles privées subventionnées est exercée par l'État; elle ne peut s'étendre au cours de religion et de morale. . . .

By virtue of the law the communal authorities do not even have a right of supervision over such schools, since the right of inspection is reserved to the central government. Communal authorities have only an indirect control, in so far as they can always bring alleged abuses to the attention of the central authorities.

But, while the general law grants to the communes this very limited power, there is nothing to prevent school committees and communes from mutually agreeing on a contract that would give wider powers to the communal administration in return for greater facilities for the school committee.

The fifth condition of adoption concerns the free character of the school attendance. No school can become legally adopted unless the instruction given in it is, at least to a certain degree, free to all.[23]

Under the present law, admission to an adopted school is always free, unless certain families voluntarily give up this right and agree on paying a certain fee to the school of their choice. Books and other equipment, however, must always be provided without cost, at least to those children whose parents' income does not, according to the records of the bureau of revenues, reach a certain level.

It devolves to communal authorities and school committees to decide whether their finances permit them to do more than this legally imposed minimum, and thus to give free equipment to all the children, regardless of the financial status of the parents. And it is exactly here that some communal councils find an opportunity to indulge in some kind of discrimination. Disposing of the money of the local taxpayers they provide free equipment for all the

---

[23] *Art. 16.*—L'instruction primaire est gratuite pour tous les enfants dans les écoles communales, adoptées et adoptables.

Toutefois, là où il est pourvu aux nécessités de l'enseignement gratuit par un nombre suffisant d'écoles ou de classes gratuites, des enfants payants peuvent être admis dans les classes ou les écoles à déterminer, le cas échéant, par les authorités communales pour les écoles communales et par les directeurs des écoles adoptées et adoptables pour ces écoles. . . .

La gratuité comporte la fourniture des objets classiques aux enfants dont les parents ne sont pas imposables à l'impôt complémentaire personnel instauré par l'article premier de l'arrêté royal du 22 février 1935. . . .

children attending the communal school, thus penalizing adopted confessional schools. These latter, thus faced with an unfair competition from another school system, and in order to give likewise free equipment to all the children, are then forced to depend on voluntary contributions and to organize lotteries, etc., which by the laws of December 31, 1851 and December 19, 1864, are legalized for all institutions of learning. One must admit, however, that this type of discrimination by some communal authorities has never become a serious threat to the confessional schools in Belgium.

c) The duration of the adoption.

A word about this legal adoption of private and denominational schools must relate to its duration.

If the school contract is signed without any specific mention of the time length, a commune can always revoke this adoption at the end of each school year, but the revocation takes effect only after one year.

Most school contracts, however, are signed for a legal maximum period of six years, at the end of which it can be renewed for a further period. And, of course, a school contract can always be ended at any time if both parties agree to do so.

3. The Adoptable School

Besides the communal, the independent, and the adopted schools, the Belgian law provides for a fourth category of elementary schools, the so-called "adoptable schools," sometimes referred to as "private subsidized schools."[24] Such are the private or denominational institutions that are not adopted by the communal authorities but have all the qualifications for such adoption, except that religious instruction is not made a compulsory subject of the curriculum.

The optional character of religious instruction in these schools could easily lead one to believe that this type of school must in

---

[24] The technical term in the legislation is *école adoptable, aanneembare school.*

practice be the anti-religious "school without God." Nothing is less true, however, since only a few anti-religious elementary schools in the country enjoy this status. Most adoptable schools, on the contrary, are just private or denominational schools, the controlling authorities of which prefer total independence from local civil authorities to the small financial advantages that adoption would bring to their teachers.

For the teachers, of course, adoption usually means a salary slightly above the State minimum and also better provisions for payments of benefits in case of sickness or retirement. But apart from that, the financial status of an adoptable school is practically not much different from that of an adopted one. Articles 22 and 23 of the law of 1919 indeed make sure that both State and provincial subsidies are extended to the adoptable schools as well as to the schools adopted by the communes. This is why the status of the adoptable school has been selected by many confessional school committees within the last few years.[25] An added reason for this is that some "friendly" communal councils now make provision in their annual budgets so that the adoptable schools will get the same financial assistance that is granted by contract to the adopted schools.[26]

This practical equality of the adopted and adoptable schools has brought some authors to question the further utility of the whole adoption system in the present Belgian school legislation. They suggest the elimination of the entire adoption procedure, with the consequent retention of only two types of subsidized elementary schools: communal public schools, and subsidized private or de-

---

[25] In 1947 there were in Belgium 1,260 such adoptable schools against 2,322 adopted and 5,114 communal schools. It must be noted, however, that many communal schools in Belgium are thoroughly Catholic schools, as will be explained later in this study. But, regardless of the religious or a-religious character of communal public elementary schools, the number of pupils attending them (337,653) is still below the number of pupils attending adopted or adoptable Catholic schools (437,725). Cf. *L'Enseignement libre,* IX (1949), 169.

[26] Cf. Bellière, *Comment administrer une Commune* (3. ed., Thuillies: Ed. Ramgal, 1946).

nominational schools, all under the control of the central government.[27]

From personal contacts, however, the writer has gathered that most teachers in the Belgian Catholic schools prefer by far the status of the adopted school to that of the adoptable. Under the system of adoption their financial regime is practically as good as that of their colleagues in the communal schools. Under the adoption system communal subsidies and services to the school are granted by contract for the whole duration of the adoption period, which is usually six years. On the other hand, adoptable schools depend for these on the fluctuating annual budgets of the communes, not to speak of the always possible psychological and political changes in the voting majority of the communal councils.

It is of course true that these advantages of the adoption are paid for normally when the communal councils have been given some indirect legal and moral authority over otherwise independent schools. But even that fact has in most localities resulted in no harm at all, but rather in very effective co-operation between civil and ecclesiastical authorities, for the ultimate benefit of the children of the people.

If the Catholic schools did not make any use of this privilege of legal adoption, inasmuch as they do not want to be even indirectly controlled by the local civil authorities, they would be putting themselves in the dangerous position of having to bow to the authority of the central government as adoptable schools, and thus leave the way open for themselves to be treated little by little as merely "national" governmental schools.

C. PUBLIC FUNDS FOR DENOMINATIONAL SCHOOLS

The question of free school attendance and free equipment for the pupils, which was treated earlier in this study, is only one aspect of the financial setup of the confessional schools in Belgium. The general principle in this matter is that the expenses of the denominational schools should be borne by the governing bodies of these schools themselves.

---

[27] Cf. Bauwens, *Code de l'Enseignement primaire,* pp. 82-83.

But civil authorities in Belgium readily admit that it is one of their principal duties to promote public instruction. They know also that under the inspection of the central government the education given in the adopted denominational schools is second to none. At the same time they are realistic enough to understand how this denominational school system saves the State a tremendous amount of money which otherwise for the education of that section of the population would have to be taken from the public taxes. Consequently, the legislator has deemed it just and proper that civil authorities share the burden of the expenses of these recognized adopted or adoptable confessional schools. This is actually done in the form of subsidies from the State, the province, and eventually also the commune.

The central government gives its support to the adopted and adoptable school by paying in full the official minimum salary of all duly appointed teaching personnel.[28] Probably to avoid the accusation of non-Catholics that the school law would thus give too much money to Catholic convents, article 30, paragraph D, states that the salary of teachers who are members of religious orders and congregations is to be only half of that of lay teachers.[29] Although Catholic Nuns and Brothers in Belgium continue to accept this discrimination without protest, it is surprising that such a specification is retained in the legislation when it can please only those who in other circumstances try to justify their anti-Catholic and anti-family policy with the slogan, "the same work calls for the same salary."

The provincial authorities will send to the communes the funds necessary to supply free equipment for those pupils who are entitled to it in communal, adopted, and adoptable schools.[30]

---

[28] *Art. 23.*—Les subventions que l'État accorde annuellement aux communes et aux directions des écoles adoptables pour le soutien, respectivement des écoles primaires communales et adoptées et des écoles primaires adoptables, sont équivalentes aux traitements du personnel enseignant, . . .

[29] *Art. 30, D.*—Le traitement des instituteurs, non mariés vivant en commun, des écoles communales, adoptées et adoptables est fixé à la moitié du traitement prévu pour les instituteurs laics.

[30] *Art. 22.*—. . . La province intervient dans les dépenses résultant de la délivrance gratuite des fournitures classiques dans les écoles primaires et gardiennes communales, adoptées ou adoptables, . . . Cf. p. 108 of this study.

The communes on their part must provide for each adopted or adoptable school the same medical inspection as for the communal public schools. Although the medical inspectors for the adopted and adoptable schools are appointed by the school committees, the commune will pay their legal salary, and also place at their disposal the necessary equipment for an effective inspection. Individual medical examination of pupils is obligatory at the time of enrollment and after that annually; moreover, a monthly visit to each class is also required.[31]

Depending on the good will and the financial status of the communal authorities, some school contracts provide also certain extra communal subsidies, such as funds for augmenting the minimum legal salary of the teachers, funds for the heating of school buildings, the establishment of a school library, the distribution of prizes, the organization of excursions, etc. And here again there is open a way by which some anti-religious communal authorities discriminate against confessional schools. Particularly, while doing so for the communal public school teachers, they refuse to add anything to the minimum State salary for the teachers in the adopted confessional schools, hoping in this way to attract the greater talents for the non-confessional schools.

It thus becomes evident that, to enjoy freedom and independence, the adopted and adoptable denominational schools in Belgium have still to pay a high price, since the erection and maintenance of school buildings and the complete furnishing of classrooms make a great demand on the financial resources and the energy of the faithful. But, Belgian parents have up to now

---

[31] *Art. 45.*—Toute commune est tenue d'établir un service gratuit d'inspection médicale scolaire, comprenant un examen des élèves au moment de leur entrée à l'école et au moins une visite mensuelle de l'école.

Ce service s'étend à toutes les écoles soumises au régime de la présente loi.

Les médecins-inspecteurs des écoles communales sont nommés par le conseil communal; les médecins-inspecteurs des écoles adoptées et adoptables sont nommée par la direction de ces établissements et agréés par le collège échevinal, sauf recours au Roi en cas de refus d'agréation, . . . Cf. Colet, *Texte commenté de la Loi des Finances provinciales et communales* (Bruxelles: Union des Villes et Communes belges, 1949).

always been ready to pay that price to maintain the schools they want for their children.[32]

D. SCHOOL AID TO CHILDREN

From all the above mentioned official subsidies to schools the Belgian law clearly distinguishes the so-called "school aid" to children, such as providing food, clothing, transportation, recreational facilities, etc.

When private organizations themselves either take the initiative in making available such school aid, or hold themselves responsible for the allocation of it, then they have a right to decide who shall benefit by it.

But if the civil authorities take the initiative, or if they in any way handle or distribute this school aid, then the law leaves no doubt as to who shall benefit by the school aid: The King himself, through his Minister, is responsible for seeing that every child, irrespective of the school he attends, benefit from this aid.[33] Such school aid is considered by the legislator as given, not to the school, but to the pupils. For especially when anything affects innocent children, Belgians, Catholics and non-Catholics alike, believe in applying article 6 of their Constitution, which states that all Belgians are equal before the law.[34]

---

[32] The highest authority over the Catholic elementary school system in Belgium is vested in the *Conseil central de l'Enseignement primaire catholique* under the immediate supervision of the hierarchy represented by a vicar-general from each diocese. This council is the official mouthpiece of the Catholic school system in its dealings with the civil authorities of the country.

[33] *Art. 46.*—. . . Les délibérations des conseils provinciaux et communaux relatives à l'organisation de réfectoires scolaires, de colonies scolaires, de distributions d'aliments ou de vêtements aux enfants des écoles, de subventions pour ces oeuvres, sont soumises à l'approbation du Roi.

Le Roi veille à ce qu'il ne soit fait, entre les enfants appelés à bénéficier de ces délibérations, aucune distinction suivant la catégorie d'écoles qu'ils fréquentent. . . .

[34] Cf. *Annales parlementaires, Chambre des Représentants,* session législative ordinaire de 1913-1914, pp. 788-819.

Typical are the statements made by the Socialist leaders in the Parliament: "Elle n'a rien de politique cette question, et il serait déplorable de l'envisager sous l'angle de nos querelles habituelles. . . . Je ne comprends pas qu'en

E. RELIGIOUS INSTRUCTION IN CIVIL PUBLIC SCHOOLS

Although the drawing up of the curriculum for communal public schools is the privilege of the communal council, article 17 of the general school law of 1919, determines the different subjects that must always be part of this curriculum. And the first compulsory subject thus mentioned in the law is instruction in religion and morality.[85] Religious and moral instruction is therefore in Belgium an integral part of the curriculum in all elementary schools administered or adopted by the civil authorities. Only the so-called adoptable schools do not have to give religious and moral instruction, in order to qualify for subsidies from both the State and the province.[86]

This Belgian school law does not discriminate against any religion. The dogmatic and moral instruction to be given in any civil public school will therefore be in the religion of the majority of the pupils. The law fully recognizes the rights of the Church as the only one qualified to teach religion and morals to its members. Art. 17, paragraph 4, therefore states most clearly that the ministers of different denominations must be invited by the proper school authorities to give religious instruction in the civil public or adopted schools.[87]

---

pareille matière on puisse se diviser selon ses opinions politiques. . . ."—Destrée, p. 794. "Si l'on peut concevoir à la rigueur que le capitalisme exploite les hommes adultes, il est inconcevable, il est intolérable qu'on laisse dans la géhenne de pauvres enfants, qu'ils soient fils de catholiques, de libéraux ou de socialistes."—Huysmans, p. 799.

The Catholic viewpoint was expressed by the Minister of Justice, Carton de Wiart: "Vis-à-vis des institutions publiques, les enfants pauvres, qui ont les mêmes besoins, ont les mêmes droits." p. 795.

[85] *Art. 17.*—L'instruction primaire comprend nécessairement l'enseignement de la religion et de la morale, . . .

[86] Cf. supra, pp. 109-110. As confirmed once more by Ministerial order of October 2, 1950, activities with a religious educational character may legally be included in the program of the civil public kindergartens, although the law itself does not make this obligatory.

[87] *Art. 17, paragraph 4.*—Les ministres des divers cultes sont invités à donner, dans les écoles primaires soumises au régime de la présente loi, l'enseignement de la religion et de la morale, ou à le faire donner, sous leur surveillance, soit par l'instituteur, s'il y consent, soit par une personne agréée par le conseil communal.

Three possibilities are now left open by the law. First of all, a minister of religion may be designated by his superiors to give this instruction himself, and he need not be a local clergyman.

In other cases the minister of religion may request the regular school teacher to take care of this religious and moral instruction as a delegate of the clergy. The teacher may accept this delegation, if he so desires, without having to ask a special authorization from the communal authorities. Once he accepts, he is for this part of his teaching under the control of the clergy. In practice this means that it is within the province of the Church authorities to take all the measures necessary for the efficient organization of this course, such as the classification of the pupils, and the selection of the textbooks. The clergyman has also the right to be present at all religious lessons given by the communal teacher, and he may, when necessary, supplement his teaching. He must not, however, pass any comments to the teacher in the presence of the pupils. The law also gives to the clergy the right to punish children for breaches of discipline during the class. Once he has agreed to teach religion, the communal teacher is not thereby compelled to do so for the whole school year, but he may withdraw at any time if he so desires. If, however, a teacher refuses to give the course in religion, he is nevertheless bound to be present at it in order to supervise the children, should the minister of religion so desire it.

There is yet another way in which the clergy can secure religious instruction in the civil public schools, namely by delegating a lay person who is not a member of the school staff. Such a delegate must be formally presented to the communal authorities who within a month will notify the clergy of their acceptance or nonacceptance. Communal authorities, however, have no right to pass judgment on the qualifications of this lay person as a teacher of religion; they are only empowered to refuse his recognition when there are serious doubts as to his uprightness of character. Such a lay person, when he has been duly delegated by the Church authorities and recognized by the commune, is entitled to a legally fixed salary, two-thirds of which must be paid by the commune and one-third by the central government. Ministers of religion and regular teachers, however, are not entitled to a salary for their course in religion, but the communal authorities may, if they think fit and it be financially possible, make to them a grant from communal funds.

Although a course in religion and morality is mandatory in all communal and adopted public schools, no pupil in a civil public school can be compelled to follow it. The decision in this matter rests exclusively with the parents whose written demand suffices for the exemption of their children from this course, provided however, that the parents make this demand freely, without any provocation by either communal or school authorities.[88]

Such a legal exemption for even one pupil will affect the whole character of a class, inasmuch as the formal course in religion must then be restricted to thirty minutes daily and must be given either at the beginning or at the close of the school hours, in order that all the children be enabled to assist conveniently at the other courses of the curriculum. A ministerial reply in Parliament made it clear however that, if in a class no one be exempted from the course in religion, communal and ecclesiastical authorities may agree to prolong this course for more than thirty minutes daily and have it at any convenient time. Such a case occurs in most rural communities where the communal public school is in practice a truly confessional Catholic school according to the wishes of the totally Catholic population.[89]

But when in classes even one pupil is exempted, the general instruction can no longer be regarded as confessional. For such classes in particular, article 21 reminds the teacher to abstain in his instruction from attacking the religious or philosophical convictions of the families of the children entrusted to his care. The same article of the law, however, insists that, even if the general education of a class can no longer proceed strictly along confes-

---

[88] *Art. 17, paragraph 6.*—Sont dispensés d'y assister, les enfants dont les parents en font la demande expresse dans les termes suivants: "Le soussigné . . . , usant du droit que lui confère l'article 17 de la loi sur l'enseignement primaire, déclare dispenser son enfant d'assister au cours de religion et dc morale."

[89] Cf. *Annales parlementaires, Chambre des Représentants,* session législative ordinaire de 1935-1936, pp. 1026-1030.

sional lines, the teacher always has the duty of inculcating the general moral standards of the nation: a sense of duty, a love for the country, a respect for the national institutions, and an attachment to the constitutional freedoms.[40] But the Minister of Public Instruction declared on another occasion in Parliament that, notwithstanding exemptions from the religious course, communal authorities have always the right to retain crucifixes or other religious emblems in their schools, if this is wanted by the majority of the parents.[41]

The inspection of religious instruction in civil public schools is left entirely to the heads of the different religious denominations, who are obliged to follow the conditions specified in article 19 of the basic school law.[42] In applying this law, religious and civil authorities conjointly have set up for the whole country three independent inspection boards respectively for Catholic, Protestant, and Jewish children.

The system of inspection for Catholic children, who make up the great majority in the communal public schools, was definitely delineated by royal decree of March 28, 1929, which was only a complement of the former decrees of December 12, 1895, and of

---

[40] *Art. 21.*—L'instituteur s'occupe avec une égale sollicitude de l'éducation et de l'instruction des enfants confiés à ses soins. Il ne néglige aucune occasion d'inculquer à ses élèves les préceptes de la morale, de leur inspirer le sentiment du devoir, l'amour de la patrie, le respect des institutions nationales, l'attachement aux libertés constitutionnelles. Il s'abstient, dans son enseignement, de toute attaque contre les personnes ou contre les convictions religieuses des familles dont les enfants lui sont confiés.

[41] Cf. *Annales parlementaires, Chambre des Représentants,* session législative ordinaire de 1935-1936, pp. 1026-1030.

[42] *Art. 19.*—L'inspection de l'enseignement de la religion et de la morale est exercée par les délégués des chefs des cultes; ces délégués remplissent leur mission dans les conditions à déterminer par un arrêté royal.

Les chefs des cultes notifient la nomination de leurs délégués au ministre de l'instruction publique, qui, après en avoir donné acte, transmet les informations nécessaires aux administrations provinciales et communales, ainsi qu'aux inspecteurs de l'enseignement primaire.

Tous les ans, au mois d'octobre, chacun des chefs des cultes adresse au ministre de l'instruction publique, un rapport détaillé sur la manière dont l'enseignement de la religion et de la morale est donné dans les écoles soumises au régime de la présente loi.

August 14, 1897.[43] Under this system the law recognizes State subsidized inspectors for the different provinces and districts. These ecclesiastical officials, or their delegates, have the right to inspect at any time the religious education in any State subsidized school, and must do so at least once a year. The report on their visits will be sent directly and only to the bishops who will then furnish an annual comprehensive survey of religious and moral instruction to the central government.[44]

What judgment then may be rendered on the present day Belgian legislation concerning the elementary schools? In answering this question the writer makes his own the words of His Eminence Joseph-Ernest Cardinal Van Roey, Archbishop of Malines, who in 1948 publicly stated that the situation in Belgium, both before and after the second World-War, can be considered as "satisfactory, although in some respects not fully answering the just claims of Catholics."[45]

It cannot be questioned that the Belgian elementary school legislation does not represent that perfect ideal that one could dream of according to the strict Catholic principles already explained in the first part of this study. In Belgium, indeed, Catholics are still bearing alone the whole burden of erecting and furnishing their own schools, while at the same time they pay taxes out of which schools are erected which will never be used by them and sometimes used against them. Likewise there are many loopholes in the present legislation, which still permits anti-Cath-

---

[43] Cf. Bauwens, *Code de l'Enseignement primaire,* pp. 177-179.

[44] Besides these diocesan and district inspectors of religion, all of them priests who inspect both civil and ecclesiastical schools, the Catholic hierarchy in Belgium appoints also lay inspectors who are responsible for examining the technical side of education in Catholic schools only, independently of the government inspectors with jurisdiction over both civil and ecclesiastical adopted or adoptable schools.

[45] ". . . notre situation scolaire, bien qu'elle ne répondit pas sous certains aspects aux légitimes exigences des catholiques, pouvait dans son ensemble paraître satisfaisante, et nous l'avons toujours acceptée sans récrimination. L'enseignement primaire était régi par une loi sur laquelle tous les partis s'étaient mis d'accord."—Cf. *L'Enseignement libre,* IX (1949), 100. Cf. also Leclef, *Le Cardinal Van Roey et l'Occupation allemande en Belgique* (Bruxelles: Ad. Goemaere, 1945).

olic local governments to engage in a subtle underhand discrimination even against legally adopted schools, as was duly pointed out above. But, even the fact that Catholics are compelled to be the principal financial supporters of their own schools does not after all seem wholly objectionable. On the contrary, in a measure one may consider it quite acceptable. The sacrifices made by Catholics for their schools do not only justify the relative freedom and independence of these institutions, but make these schools so much more a part of their own heritage, for these schools become the more valued and appreciated as a consequence of the daily sacrifices and energy that make their existence possible.

Besides, small details which can be rightly criticized should not make anyone overlook the brighter side of the present Belgian elementary school system. Having studied this system thoroughly in both its theoretical setup and practical application, the writer has gained the firm conviction that to many countries where the useless school controversy still antagonizes citizens the Belgian system could bring an equitable solution, for, more than any other system, it appears to be a successful synthesis of the educational rights of families, Church, and State.

It would be hard to imagine a school legislation in which the *rights of the parents,* as the first and principal educators, are more respected. Not only does the Constitution give everyone the right to establish and administer private schools in total independence, but the whole setup of the public elementary school system is removed from the direct control of any central government, and placed entirely in the hands of the local civil authorities, who can rightly be considered the immediate representatives of the fathers and mothers who elected them. The fact that the parents of only twenty school children can effectively call upon the local communities to provide them with the kind of school they prefer speaks for itself. Likewise, upholding the sound philosophy that true education must be based on religious and moral principles, the State insists that religious and moral instruction be made a compulsory part of the curriculum of all civil public schools. But at the same time the rights of conscience of all parents are fully respected, since not even one single child can be forced to be indoctrinated with religious or philosophical ideas alien to the wishes of his parents.

Catholics therefore should think twice before departing in the slightest from this sanctioned principle of local autonomy for the elementary schools. Not only for reasons of financial gain, but more so for motives based on sound principles, they should reject all the specious arguments of those who question the utility in our days of the adoption system and would entirely replace it with that of merely adoptable schools. Even more categorically should they reject the completely illegal and unconstitutional moves of those who, like the Socialist Camille Huysmans immediately after World-War II, try to "nationalize" the whole educational system. The Belgian legislation, indeed, gives absolutely no power to the central government in the matter of setting up an elementary school system, so that even the idea of a "national primary school" must be excluded under the present legislation.[46]

A legislation that so highly respects the religious and philosophical convictions of the parents will most logically also guarantee the *rights of the Church* under whose care these parents place the education of their children. Denominational confessional schools therefore appear in the Belgian legislation first of all as institutions demanded by the parents, and then as institutions directed by Church authorities. This becomes even more evident when one considers the total equality enjoyed by all religious denominations. As far as the educational rights of the Catholic Church are concerned, one must say that the Belgian elementary school legislation fully recognizes the Church as the only qualified teacher of religion and morality for its members, and acknowledges this right with all the practical consequences included in this principle.

And yet, while most fully respecting parental and ecclesiastical rights in the field of education, the civil authorities, and the central

---

[46] Not only the Catholics in Parliament defended this viewpoint, but also the *Cour des Comptes,* the official body set up to control the expenses made by the government, confirmed this interpretation in 1948 against the action of the Socialist cabinet Spaak-Huysmans. Cf. du Bus de Warnaffe, "Les Droits constitutionnels du Ministère de l'instruction publique," *L'Enseignement libre,* IX (1949), 161.

government in particular, still have over public education that degree of *control* which every *modern State* can justly claim.

In laying down a definite curriculum for all communal and State subsidized schools, and in requiring strict professional training for all licensed teachers, the central government has every guarantee that the technical and civil education of the young citizens is fully provided for.

Differing from the authoritarian State that makes itself absolute, even in the field of education, the Belgian State recognizes that its part in elementary education is only a secondary and subsidiary one. Consequently it declares itself ready to support each and every school that measures up to its educational standards and is willing to accept its inspection.

This typical Belgian system of "subsidized liberty" is not only a truly democratic way of using public taxes for the benefit of all citizens, regardless of their religious opinions, but the granting of these subsidies is also a sound economical policy, for by fostering the initiative of the Church the government sees this latter erect schools which otherwise the State would have to provide.

Readily admitting that there is room for improvement in some small details of the Belgian elementary school system and that the true spirit of this legislation has not been faithfully kept by some partisan officials, the writer nevertheless sincerely thinks that, from the Catholic viewpoint, the ones responsible for this school system deserve the gratitude and admiration of Catholic citizens. Adapting the words that Leo XIII, of glorious memory, once pronounced in regard to the Belgian Constitution, one may venture to say at the end of this study: The works of men are by no means perfect. Thus it is with the Belgian elementary school legislation. But the state of Catholicity in Belgium, after forty years of experience and despite the moral devastations of two World Wars, proves that in the modern society the Belgian system of subsidized liberty is very well suited to the needs of the Church. The Belgian Catholics must therefore uphold their present system.

Not only from the Catholic viewpoint, but also from the national angle, the present school system in both communal and denominational schools has proved to be very effective. It is common knowledge that the education provided in Belgium's schools can stand comparison with that of any other country. And the fact that even in the official civil public schools religion has been given the first place among the compulsory subjects is certainly not the least influencing factor in safeguarding the high moral standards of the country.

And as far as regards its international significance, the Belgian elementary school system stands, in a world of frictions and conflicts of all kinds, as a living proof that school controversies among citizens of the same nation can be avoided, and that an equitable solution for the school problem can be found in harmonious co-ordination of the rights and duties of families, Church, and State.

In particular, those people who in certain countries still maintain that Catholicism is finally aiming at the totalitarian imposition of its views upon all the members of the nation should look into and meditate upon the Belgian elementary school system. There is a country where still the overwhelming majority of the citizens are members of the Catholic Church; where that Church can at the present day even rely on a favorable political majority in both Houses of Parliament and a totally Catholic government. In such a country, and under such circumstances, Catholics insist on maintaining a school legislation that actually does not give the Catholic Church any privileged status, but sanctions equality and freedom for all religious and philosophical convictions. Belgium thus shows to the whole world a Catholic way of bringing peace and unity into the most important field of the public life of a nation: the elementatry education of its children.

CONCLUSIONS

1. To refer to the official Catholic Schools as if they were private schools is to disregard the fact that these Catholic schools are erected by the public authority of a juridically self-contained perfect society.

2. The Church may not have the right to appoint teachers of religion in strictly private schools, but the Church has certainly and in all circumstances the right and the duty to demand its positive approbation for all teachers of the Catholic religion.

3. Never has the Church claimed a monopoly in education. But, when existing schools do not guarantee the proper training of Catholic youth, then a Catholic School System becomes a necessity.

4. Although its rôle must be entirely secondary, the State has specific rights and duties in the field of education.

5. Only when the combined activities of families and Church fall short of providing a complete system of public education has the State the duty and the right to organize its own School System in addition to existing private or denominational schools.

6. However general its disapproval of neutral or mixed schools may be, the Church has never intended to blame the Catholic teachers in such schools.

7. The letter of Archbishop de Méan, read to the members of the Belgian National Congress on December 17, 1830, cannot be described as an unwarranted encroachment on the domain of the State. What is more, the great importance of this episcopal intervention rest precisely in the fact that there for the first time in Belgian history a responsible Churchman renounced all the privileges of the "old regime."

8. In the views of the majority that sanctioned the Belgian Constitution of 1831 freedom of education is not only the logical consequence of freedom of religion, but is primarily based upon the natural rights of the family. Consequently, in the Belgian

Constitution the educational rôle of the State is only secondary and merely subsidiary.

9. The first law organizing the elementary schools in Belgium, the law of 1842, should not be called a law of unity, "une loi unioniste," but rather a law of compromise.

10. In 1842 Archbishop Sterckx was right in bringing out the need for some kind of law concerning the elementary schools in Belgium. The actual conditions of the time called for such legal intervention, and, moreover, so-called juridical objections were mere assertions with no foundation in fact.

11. The particular school law of 1842 should not have received the support of the Catholics, since it was from the outset nothing else than a political trap which would necessarily prove fatal to them.

12. The tragic mistake of Archbishop Sterckx in 1842 was that by seeking to bring all civil public schools into the hands of the Church he opened the way for that same Church to lose its own schools.

13. The mistake made by an Archbishop in 1842 was repeated by a Liberal Minister forty years later: Just as Sterckx lost his own Catholic institutions by trying to take over all civil public schools, so by attempting to eliminate all religious schools Van Humbeeck ruined the civil public school system.

14. The characteristics of the "law of misfortune" of 1879 are: complete secularization of education, and the supreme educational jurisdiction of the central government.

15. The Belgian hierarchy of 1879 was absolutely right in condemning most vigorously the "law of misfortune" as being a systematic attack against religion in general, and against the Catholic Church in particular. By mobilizing all Catholic forces against a government defying the majority of the people, the Belgian bishops laid the foundations for the now flourishing Catholic school system.

16. Although non-Catholic historians still continue to refer to the Belgian government of 1895 as an openly clerical cabinet,

the educational policy of this government proved its desire to respect all religious and philosophical opinions.

17. The proposed system of the "school coupon" of 1911 coordinated harmoniously the educational rights of the family, of the Church, and of the State, and could have brought the Belgian school controversy to a just end.

18. The present Belgian school law distinguishes clearly "subsidies to schools" from "school aid to children," which is considered by the legislator as given, not to the school, but to the children, irrespective of the school they attend.

19. Despite the practical equality of both "adopted" and "adoptable" schools in many localities, the legal status of the adopted school must be preferred under the present Belgian "system of subsidized liberty."

20. Apart from small details which can be rightly criticized, the present Belgian elementary school system could bring an equitable solution to many countries where the school controversy still divides the citizens, for, more than any other system, it offers a successful synthesis of the educational rights of the families, the Church, and the State.

BIBLIOGRAPHY[1]

Sources

Acta Apostolicae Sedis, Commentarium Officiale, Romae, 1909—

Acta et Decreta Concilii Plenarii Baltimorensis Tertii (1884), Baltimorae, 1886.

Acta et Decreta Concilii Provincialis Mechliniensis Quarti (1922), Mechliniae: Dessain, 1923.

Acta et Decreta Concilii Provincialis Mechliniensis Quinti (1937), Mechliniae: Dessain, 1938.

Acta et Decreta Conciliorum Recentiorum (Collectio Lacensis), 7 vols., Friburgi Brisgoviae, 1870-1892.

Acta Sanctae Sedis, 41 vols., Romae, 1865-1908.

Alvin, *Discussion sur la Loi de l'Instruction primaire du 23 septembre 1842,* d'après le Moniteur Belge, précédée d'une introduction historique et des documents principaux antérieurs aux débats publics, Bruxelles, 1843.

Annales Parlementaires, Parlementaire Handelingen, Bruxelles, 1848—

Annuaire Statistique de la Belgique et du Congo Belge, Bruxelles: Ministère de l'Intérieur, 1870—

Assemblée générale des Catholiques en Belgique, 5 vols., Bruxelles, 1864, 1865, 1868.

Bartels, Adolphe, *Documents historiques sur la Révolution belge,* 2. ed., Bruxelles-La Haye: T. Lejeune, 1836.

Le Belgique et le Vatican. Documents et Travaux législatifs concernant la Rupture des Relations diplomatiques entre le Gouvernement belge et le Saint-Siège, précédés d'un Exposé historique des Rapports qui ont existé entre eux depuis 1830, 3 vols., ed. A. Banning, Bruxelles: Bruylant-Christophe & Cie, 1880-1881.

Belgische Grondwet, Gemeentewet, Provinciale Wet, met Aanduiding der wetgevende en door het Reglement voorgeschreven Schikkingen die er Betrekking op hebben, Brussel: E. Guyot, 1944.

Berta, J.-Vanderveld, E., *Code des Lois politiques et administratives,* 3 vols., 3. ed., Bruxelles: Bruylant, 1929.

[1] It is not here the writer's intention to give an exhaustive bibliography on the subject of this study, as this would be tantamount to a bibliography of the whole political and religious history of Belgium. He is therefore mentioning here only these sources and works he actually consulted and which have influenced in one way or another the stand he takes in this essay, even if they were not quoted in the text of the dissertation itself.

Biographie nationale, 28 vols., Bruxelles: Académie royale de Belgique, 1866-1944.

Bouscaren, T. Lincoln, *The Canon Law Digest,* 2 vols., and Supplement through 1948, Milwaukee: Bruce, 1934, 1943, 1949.

Bruns, V., *Fontes Iuris Gentium,* Series B., sectio I, Tomus I, Répertoire de la Correspondance des États européens, 1856-1871, Pars I, fasc. 1-2, Berlin, 1932.

Buffin, Camille, *Mémoires et Documents inédits sur la Révolution belge et la Campagne des Dix-Jours,* 1830-1831, 2 vols., Bruxelles: Kiesling-Imbreghts, 1912.

Bulletin du Ministère de l'Instruction publique, Bruxelles, 1879-1884, and 1929—

Bulletin du Ministère de l'Intérieur et de l'Instruction publique, 23 vols., Bruxelles, 1884-1907.

Bulletin du Ministère des Sciences et des Arts, 22 vols., Bruxelles, 1907-1929.

Cambier, J. F., *Recueil général de la Jurisprudence belge, 1926-1935,* Bruxelles: F. Larcier, 1937.

Canones et Decreta Sacrosancti Oecumenici Concilii Tridentini, Romae: Typographia Polyglotta S.C. de Propaganda Fide, 1882.

Codes Edmond Picard en Concordance avec les Pandectes belges, 2. ed., Bruxelles: F. Larcier, 1928.

Codex Iuris Canonici, Pii X. Pontificis Maximi iussu digestus Benedicti Papae XV auctoritate promulgatus, Romae: Typis Polyglottis Vaticanis, 1917.

Codicis Iuris Canonici Fontes, cura Emī Petri Card. Gasparii editi, 9 vols., Romae (postea Civitate Vaticana): Typis Polyglottis Vaticanis, 1923-1939. (Vols. VII-IX ed. cura et studio Emī Iustiniani Card. Serédi.)

Collectio Epistolarum Pastoralium, Decretorum aliorumque Documentorum, quae pro Regimine Dioecesis Mechliniensis publicata fuerunt, 3 vols., Mechliniae, 1845-1870.

de Gerlache, Etienne-Constantin, *Histoire du Royaume des Pays-Bas depuis 1814 jusqu'en 1830,* précédée d'un coup d'oeil sur les grandes époques de la civilisation belge, et suivie d'un essai sur l'histoire du Royaume de Belgique depuis la Révolution de 1830 jusqu'aujourd'hui, accompagnée de discours parlementaires, de notes et de pièces justificatives, 3 vols., 2. ed., Bruxelles: M. Hayez, 1842.

Denzinger, Heinrich-Bannwart, Clemens et Umberg, Johannes, *Enchiridion Symbolorum, Definitionum, et Declarationum de Rebus Fidei et Morum,* 21.-23. ed., Friburgi Brisgoviae: Herder & Co., 1937.

Enquête scolaire, 5 vols., Bruxelles: Chambre des Représentants-Commission d'enquête scolaire, 1881-1883.

Enquête sur la Condition des Classes ouvrières et sur le Travail des Enfants, 3 vols., Bruxelles: Ministère de l'Intérieur, 1846-1848.

Hardouin, J., *Acta Conciliorum et Epistolae Decretales ac Constitutiones Summorum Pontificum,* 12 vols., Parisiis, 1714-1715.

Huyttens de Terbecq, Emile, *Discussions du Congrès National de Belgique, 1830-1831*, précédées d'une introduction et suivie de plusieurs actes relatifs au Gouvernement Provisoire, . . . 2 vols., Bruxelles: Société Typographique belge, 1844-1845.

Lo Grasso, I., *Ecclesia et Status. De Mutuis Officiis et Iuribus Fontes Selecti*, Romae, 1939.

Mansi, J. D., *Sacrorum Conciliorum Nova et Amplissima Collectio*, 53 vols., Parisiis-Arnhem-Lipsiae, 1901-1927.

Le Moniteur Belge, Belgisch Staatsblad, Bruxelles, 1831—

Pasinomie ou Collection complète des Lois. Décrets, Arrêtés et Réglements qui peuvent être invoqués en Belgique, Ie Série, 1788-1814; 2de Série, 1814-1830, Bruxelles: Bruylant-Christophe & Cie, 1833-1842.

Rapport décennal sur la Situation de l'Instruction primaire en Belgique, 1830-1840, Bruxelles: Ministère de l'Intérieur, 1842.

Rapport sur la Situation de l'Instruction primaire en Belgique, 1843-1896, 15 vols., Bruxelles: Ministère de l'Intérieur et de l'Instruction publique, 1846-1896.

Recueil des Mandements, Lettres pastorales et autres Documents publiés par S. A. le Prince M. de Broglie, Gand, 1843.

Sauveur, Jules, *Royaume de Belgique, État intellectuel.* Extrait de l'Exposé de la Situation du Royaume de 1861 à 1875, Bruxelles: Commission centrale de statistique, 1876.

Schroeder, H., *Canons and Decrees of the Council of Trent*, St. Louis: B. Herder & Co., 1941.

La Séparation de L'Église et de l'État en France. Exposé et Documents. Livre Blanc du Saint-Siège, Rome, 1905.

Simon, J.,-de Beus, P., *Belgische Strafwetten; Strafwetboek; Wetboek van Strafvordering en Bijkomende Wetten*, 2. ed., Brussel: E. Bruylant, 1938.

Situation de l'Enseignement primaire et des Oeuvres scolaires d'ordre social, Bruxelles: Ministère de l'Intérieur et de l'Instruction publique, Administration centrale de l'Enseignement primaire, 1903.

Statistique des Écoles primaires, officielles et privées, au 31 décembre 1881, Bruxelles: Chambre des Représentants-Commision d'enquête scolaire, 1883.

Statuta Dioecesis Gandavensis (in Synodo Dioecesana 1939), Gandavi: Van Fleteren, 1940.

Sylloge Praecipuorum Documentorum Recentium Summorum Pontificum et S. Congregationis de Propaganda Fide necnon aliarum SS. Congregationum Romanarum, Romae: Typis Polyglottis Vaticanis, 1939.

Van Goethem, Fernand-Victor, René, *De Belgische Wetboeken. T. I. Grondwet. Burgerlijk Wetboek*, Brussel: F. Larcier, 1940.

Van Haesendonck, Émile, *De juiste Teksten van de Belgische Grondwet, van de Gemeentewet, en van de Provinciale Wet*, Brussel: E. Guyot, 1948.

Wyvekens, Hippolyte, *Code alphabétique des Lois politiques et spéciales en vigueur en Belgique,* Bruxelles: Bruylant-Christophe & Cie, 1875.

Reference Works

Aertnys, Josephus-Damen, Cornelius, *Theologia Moralis secundum doctrinam S. Alfonsi,* 15. ed., 2 vols., Romae: Marietti, 1947.

Alphonsus Liguori, St., *Theologia Moralis,* ed. L. Gaudé, 4 vols., Romae, 1905-1912.

Aquinas, St. Thomas, *Opera Omnia,* ed. Vivès, 32 vols., Parisiis, 1871-1879; *De Eruditione Principum; De Regimine Principum; Summa Theologica.*

Axters, Henri, *Commentaire de la Loi organique de l'Intruction primaire,* Bruges: G. Claeys-Weghsteen, 1898.

Badii, C., *Ius canonicum comparatum cum Edictis Legum civilium de Re ecclesiastica,* Romae, 1925.

Balau, *Soixante-dix Ans d'Histoire contemporaine de Belgique, 1815-1884,* 4. ed., Louvain, 1890.

Baudouin, Jean M., *Rapport sur l'État actuel de l'Enseignement spécial et de l'Enseignement primaire en Belgique, en Allemagne, et en Suisse,* Paris: Imprimerie impériale, 1865.

Bauwens, Léon, *Code de l'Enseignement primaire,* 12. ed., Bruxelles: L'Édition universelle, 1949.

———, *Code de l'Enseignement primaire et de l'Enseignement normal primaire,* 12. ed., Bruxelles: L'Édition universelle, 1951.

Bayer, Henry G., *The Belgians, First Settlers in New York and in the Middle States,* with a Review of the Events which led to their Immigration, New York: The Devin-Adair Company, 1925.

Bellière, Fernand, *Comment administrer une Commune,* 3. ed., Thuillies: Ed. Ramgal, 1946.

Beltjens, Gustave, *Encyclopédie du Droit civil belge,* 8 vols., Bruxelles: Bruylant-Christophe & Cie, 1905-1908.

Bender, L., *Kerk en Staat, "De Katholieke Kerk,"* t. 37, Kortrijk: Zonnewende, 1938.

Berteloot, J., *La Franc-maçonnerie et l'Église catholique,* 2 vols., "Collection Hommes et Cités," Paris, 1945.

Bertrand, Louis, *Histoire de la Démocratie et du Socialisme en Belgique depuis 1830,* 2 vols., Bruxelles: Dechesne & Cie, 1905-1907.

Beste, Udalricus, *Introductio in Codicem,* 2. ed., Collegeville, Minn.: St. John's Abbey Press, 1944.

Billot, L., *Tractatus de Ecclesia Christi,* 2 vols., Romae: Apud Aedes Universitatis Gregorianae, 1927.

Boffa, Conrad, *Canonical Provisions for Catholic Schools,* The Catholic University of America, Canon Law Studies, n. 117, Washington, D. C.: The Catholic University of America Press, 1939.

Boon, V., *Het Belgisch Staatsrecht.* Boek I: *Het Grondwettelijk Recht,* 2. ed., 2 vols., Brussel: E. Bruylant, 1948.

Bornet, Étienne, *La Position de l'Église en face du Problème de l'École,* "L'Église expliquée aux Incroyants," Paris: Flammarion, 1943.

Bosch, A., *Essai sur la Liberté de l'Enseignement et sur les Principes généraux d'une Loi organique de l'Instruction publique,* précédé d'un coup d'oeil sur la Situation actuelle du Royaume des Pays-Pas, Bruxelles, 1829.

Bouscaren, T.-Ellis, A., *Canon Law,* Milwaukee: Bruce, 1946.

Bronne, Carlo, *Léopold Ier et son Temps,* "Le Passé," Bruxelles: A. Goemaere, 1942.

———, *Lettres de Léopold Ier, Premier Roi des Belges,* Bruxelles: C. Dessart, 1943.

Brunet, Émile-Gervais, Jean, e.a., *Répertoire pratique du Droit belge; Législation, Doctrine, et Jurisprudence,* Bruxelles: E. Bruylant, 1929.

Burns, James, *The Catholic School System in the United States; its Principles, Origin and Establishment,* New York-Cincinnati-Chicago: Benziger Brothers, 1908.

———, *The Growth and Development of the Catholic School System in the United States,* New York-Cincinnati-Chicago: Benziger Brothers, 1912.

Cappello, Felix M., *Summa Iuris Canonici,* 3 vols., Romae: Apud Aedes Universitatis Gregorianae, 1928-1934.

———, *Summa Iuris Publici Ecclesiastici,* 2. ed., Romae: Apud Aedes Universitatis Gregorianae, 1928.

Carton de Wiart, Henry, *Beernaert et son Temps,* Bruxelles: Renaissance du Livre, 1945.

———, *Souvenirs politiques,* Bruges: Desclée-De Brouwer, 1948.

Catholic Encyclopedia, The, 15 vols., Index and 2 Supplements, New York, 1907-1922.

Cathrein, Victor, *Moralphilosophie,* 2. ed., 2 vols., Freiburg im Breisgau: Herder & Co., 1893.

Chénon, E., *Histoire des Rapports de l'Église et de l'État du Ier au XXe Siècle,* Paris, 1913.

Cicognani, Amleto, *Canon Law,* 2. ed., transl. by J. O'Hara and F. Brennan, Westminster: The Newman Bookshop, 1947.

Civardi, Luigi, *A Manual of Catholic Action,* transl. by C. C. Martindale, New York: Sheed & Ward, 1936.

Claeys Boúúaert, F.-Simenon, G., *Manuale Juris Canonici, ad Usum Seminariorum,* 3 vols., Gandae-Leodii: Apud Auctores in Seminariis Gandavensi et Leodiensi, 1934-1935.

Colenbrander, Herman-Theodoor, *De Afscheiding van Belgie,* Amsterdam: J. M. Meulenhoff, 1936.

———, *Gedenkstukken der Algemeene Geschiedenis van Nederland van 1795 tot 1840, d.VII-IX* (1813-1830), 's Gravenhage: Rijks Geschiedkundige Publicatien, 1917.

——, *Willem I. Koning der Nederlanden,* 2 vols., Amsterdam: J. M. Meulenhoff, 1932.

Colet, Paul, *Texte commenté de la Loi des Finances provinciales et communales,* Bruxelles: Union des Villes et Communes belges, 1949.

Coronata, Matthaeus Conte a, *Institutiones Iuris Canonici,* 2. ed., 5 vols., Taurini-Romae: Marietti, 1939-1947.

D'Alès, A., *Dictionnaire apologétique de la Foi catholique,* 4. ed., 4 vols., Paris: Beauchesne, 1925-1931.

Dareste, F. R.-Delpech, J.-Laferrière, J., *Les Constitutions modernes,* 4. ed., Paris, 1928.

De Buck, Victor, *Les Principes catholiques et la Constitution belge,* Bruxelles: Vromant, 1878.

Dechamps, A., *Les Projets inconstitutionnels contre la Loi de 1842 ou l'École dans ses rapports avec l'État, la Religion et la Liberté,* Bruxelles, 1878.

de Dorlodot, René, *Souvenirs,* Bruxelles: A. Goemaere, 1947.

Defourny, M., *Les Congrès catholiques en Belgique,* Louvain, 1908.

de Gerlache, Étienne-Constantin, *Essai sur le Mouvement des Partis en Belgique depuis 1830 jusqu'à ce jour,* suivi de quelques réflexions sur ce qu'on appelle les grands Principes de 1789, 2. ed., Bruxelles: Aug. Decq, 1852.

de Henricourt de Grunne, *Vingt-cinq Années de Gouvernement,* Bruxelles: A. Dewit, 1910.

De Hovre, Frans, *Philosophy and Education,* transl. by E. Jordan, New York: Benziger Brothers, 1931.

de Lannoy, Fleury, *Histoire diplomatique de l'Indépendance belge, 1830-1839,* Bruxelles: Office de Publicité, 1948.

de Lichtervelde, Louis, *La Monarchie en Belgique sous Léopold Ier et Léopold II,* Paris-Bruxelles: G. Van Oest, 1921.

——, *Le Congrès National, l'Oeuvre et les Hommes,* Bruxelles: Renaissance du Livre, 1945.

——, *Leopold First, the Founder of Modern Belgium,* transl. by T. H. Reed and H. R. Reed, New York-London: The Century Co., 1930.

——, *Léopold II,* 4. ed., Bruxelles: L'Édition universelle, 1935.

Delplace, Louis, *La Belgique sous Guillaume I, Roi des Pays-Bas,* Louvain: J.-B. Istas, 1899.

Demarteau, J., *François-Antoine de Méan, dernier Prince-Évêque de Liège, premier Primat de Belgique,* Bruxelles: Office de Publicité, 1944.

De Meester, Alphonsus, *Juris Canonici et Juris Canonico-Civilis Compendium,* nova ed., 3 vols. in 4, Brugis: Desclée-De Brouwer, 1921-1928.

——, *La Liberté d'Enseignement, Étude de Droit constitutionnel,* Bruges: Desclée-De Brouwer, 1922.

de Moreau, Édouard, *Adolphe Dechamps, 1807-1875,* Bruxelles: A. Dewit, 1911.

——, *L'Église en Belgique des Origines au Début du XXe Siècle,* Bruxelles: L'Edition universelle, 1944.

Demoulin, Robert, *Guillaume Ier et la Transformation économique des Provinces belges, 1815-1830,* Liège: Bibliothèque de l'Université, 1938.

——, *Les Journées de septembre 1830 à Bruxelles et en Province,* Liège: Bibliothèque de l'Université, 1934.

de Nothomb, Jean-Baptiste, *Essai historique et politique sur la Révolution belge,* 2 vols., Bruxelles-Leipzig: C. Muquardt, 1876.

——, *État de l'Instruction primaire en Belgique, 1830-1840,* précédé d'un exposé de la législation antérieure à 1830 et suivi du texte des Lois, Arrêtés et Circulaires de 1814 à 1840, Bruxelles, 1842.

de Potter, Louis, *Révolution belge de 1828 à 1839,* 3 vols., Bruxelles: Cans & Cie, 1839.

——, *Union des Catholiques et des Libéraux,* Bruxelles: Cans & Cie, 1829.

de Reynold, Gonzague, *L'Europe tragique,* Paris: Ed. Spes, 1934.

De Schepper, Arthur-Vansiliette, Gabriel, *Wet tot Regeling van het Lager Onderwijs.* Wetgeving. Commentaar. Besluiten en Omzendbrieven, Lier: J. Van In & Co., 1948.

Destrée, Jules-Vandervelde, Émile, *Le Socialisme en Belgique,* Paris: Bibliothèque socialiste internationale, 1903.

Dewey, John, *Democracy and Education,* New York: The Macmillan Co., 1916.

Discailles, E., *Charles Rogier,* 4 vols., Bruxelles: A. Dewit, 1892-1895.

Donald, Charles, *La Situation politique et la Lutte des Partis en Belgique,* Paris: Bureaux de la Revue brittannique, 1882.

Doyle, John, *Education in Recent Constitutions and Concordats,* Washington, D. C.: The Catholic University of America, 1933.

du Bus de Warnaffe, Charles, *Physionomie du Congrès National* d'après la Correspondance de François Louis du Bus, membre du dit Congrès, Bruxelles: A. Dewit, 1930.

——, *Au Temps de l'Unionisme.* Contribution à l'étude de la Formation de l'État belge, d'après la Correspondance de François et Edmond du Bus, Tournai: Casterman, 1944.

du Bus de Warnaffe, Charles-Beyaert, C., *Le Congrès National.* Biographies des Membres du Congrès National et du Gouvernement Provisoire Belge, 1830-1831, Bruxelles: Librairie nationale d'art et d'histoire, 1931.

Ducpétiaux, Édouard, *De l'État de l'Instruction primaire et populaire en Belgique,* comparé avec celui de l'Instruction en Allemagne, en Prussie, en Suisse, en France, en Hollande, et aux États-Unis, 2 vols., Bruxelles: Meline-Caus & Cie, 1838.

——, *Quelques Mots sur l'État actuel de l'Instruction primaire en Belgique, et sur la Nécessité de l'améliorer,* Bruxelles: de Weissenbruch Père, 1839.

Dunning, W., *History of Political Theories from Rousseau to Spencer,* New York: The Macmillan Co., 1926.

Ferraris, Lucius, *Prompta Bibliotheca Canonica, Iuridica, Moralis, Theologica, necnon Ascetica, Polemica, Rubristica, Historica,* 9 vols., Romae, 1885-1899.

Gabel, Richard J., *Public Funds for Church and Private Schools,* Washington, D. C.: The Catholic University of America, 1937.

Garsou, Jules, *L'Évolution du Parti libéral à Bruxelles, 1841-1939,* Bruxelles: Imprimèrie du Marais, 1939.

Geschiedenis van Vlaanderen, onder leiding van R. van Roosbroeck, 5 vols., Antwerpen: Standaard Boekhandel, 1936-1940.

Gille, Louis-Ooms, Alphonse-Delandsheere, Paul, *Cinquante Mois d'Occupation allemande, 1914-1918,* 3 vols., Bruxelles: A. Dewit, 1919.

Giron, Alfred, *Dictionnaire de Droit administratif et de Droit public,* 3 vols., Bruxelles: Bruylant-Christophe & Cie, 1895-1896.

Goris, Jan-Albert, e.a., *Belgium.* "The United Nations Series," Robert J. Kernes general editor, Berkeley-Los Angeles: University of California Press, 1945.

Greyson, E., *L'Enseignement public en Belgique,* Aperçu historique et Exposé de la Législation, 3 vols., Bruxelles: Bibliothèque belge des Connaissances modernes, 1839-1896.

Griffin, Joseph, *The Contribution of Belgium to the Catholic Church in America, 1523-1857,* Washington, D. C.: The Catholic University of America, 1932.

Guyot de Mishaegen, G., *Le Parti catholique belge de 1830 à 1884,* Bruxelles: F. Larcier, 1946.

Harsin, P., *Essai sur l'Opinion publique en Belgique de 1815 à 1830,* Charleroi: La Terre wallonne, 1930.

Heylen, Victor, *Voor meer Rechtvaardigheid,* Bibliotheca Mechliniensis, n. 2, Brugge: Desclée-De Brouwer, 1942.

Horne, Charles-Keller, Augustus, *History of the Belgian People from the first authentic Annals to the Present Time,* New York: The International Historical Society, 1917.

Hymans, L., *Histoire parlementaire de Belgique, 1830-1910,* 9 vols., Bruxelles: Bruylant-Christophe, 1878-1910.

Janssens, Louis, *Personne et Société, Théories actuelles et Essai doctrinal,* Gembloux: J. Duculot, 1939.

Juste, Théodore, *Le Congrès National de Belgique, 1830-1831,* précédé de quelques Considérations sur la Constitution belge par Émile de Laveleye, 2 vols., Bruxelles: C. Muquardt, 1880.

——, *Essai sur l'Histoire de l'Instruction publique en Belgique,* Bruxelles: A. Jamar, 1844.

——, *Memoirs of Leopold I, King of the Belgians,* 2 vols., London: Low-Marston, 1868.

Kurth, Godefoid, "*Belgium,*" in *The Catholic Encyclopedia,* 15 vols., Index and 2 Supplements, New York, 1907-1922, II, 395-407.

Lalanne, J. A., *Influence des Pères de l'Église sur l'Éducation publique pendant les cinq premiers Siècles de l'Ère chrétienne,* Paris, 1850.

Lebeau, J., *Souvenirs personnels, 1824-1841, et Correspondance diplomatique,* Bruxelles, 1883.

Leclef, Edmond, *Le Cardinal Van Roey et l'Occupation allemande en Belgique,* Bruxelles: Ad. Goemaere, 1945.

Lecler, Joseph, *L'Église et la Souveraineté de l'État,* Paris: Ed. Flammarion, 1946.

Lexikon der Pädagogik der Gegenwart, hrsg. vom Deutschen Institut für wissenschaftliche Pädagogik, Münster i. W., Freiburg i.B., 1930-1932.

Macar, Alfred, *Cours élémentaire de Droit constitutionnel de la Belgique,* 2. ed., Liège: Vaillant-Carmanne, 1922.

Maillie, L., *La Maçonnerie belge d'après les Documents maçonniques,* Bruxelles, 1906.

Marique, Pierre J., *History of Christian Education,* 3 vols., New York: Fordham University Press, 1924-1932.

Mayence, Fernand, *La Correspondance de S. E. le Cardinal Mercier avec le Gouvernement Général allemand pendant l'Occupation 1914-1918,* Bruxelles: A. Dewit, 1919.

Merkelbach, Benedictus-Henricus, *Summa Theologiae Moralis ad Mentem D. Thomae et ad Normam Iuris Novi,* 3 vols., Parisiis; Desclée-De Brouwer, 1931-1933.

Moulart, F. J., *L'Église et l'État, ou les deux Puissances.* Leur Origine, leurs Relations, leur Droit et leurs Limites, 4. ed., Louvain: Van Linthout, 1895.

Moyersoen, Ludovic, *Prosper Poullet en de Politiek van zijn Tijd,* Brugge: Desclée-De Brouwer, 1946.

Noldin, H.-Schmitt, A., *Summa Theologica Moralis iuxta Codicem Iuris Canonici,* 26. ed., 3 vols., Oeniponte-Lipsiae: Rauch, 1939.

Oddone, Andrea, *La Costituzione Sociale della Chiesa e le sue Relazione con lo Stato,* Milano: Soc. Ed. Vita e Pensiero, 1932.

Ojetti, Benedictus, *Commentarium in Codicem Iuris Canonici,* 4 vols., Romae: Apud Aedes Universitatis Gregorianae, 1927-1931.

Orban, O., *Le Droit constitutionnel de la Belgique,* 3 vols., Liège-Paris, 1906-1911.

Ottaviani, Alaphridus, *Institutiones Iuris Publici Ecclesiastici,* 2. ed., 2 vols., Romae: Typis Polyglottis Vaticanis, 1935-1936.

Pirenne, Henri, *Histoire de Belgique,* 7 vols., Bruxelles: Lamertin, 1909-1932.

Prümmer, Dominicus, *Manuale Theologiae Moralis,* 8. ed., 3 vols., Friburgi Brisgoviae: Herder & Co., 1935-1936.

Quigley, Joseph, *Condemned Societies,* The Catholic University of America, Canon Law Studies, n. 46, Washington, D. C.: The Catholic University of America, 1927.

Reed, Thomas H., *Government and Politics of Belgium*, Yonkers-on-Hudson, N. Y.: World Book Co., 1924.

Rodenbach, Constantin, *Épisodes de la Révolution dans les Flandres, 1829, 1830, 1831*, Bruxelles: L. Hauman & Cie, 1833.

Scarascia, Giuseppe, *Le Scuole Parrocchiali e degli Istituti Religiosi e l'Istruzione Elementare in Italia*, Torino: Soc. Ed. Internazionale, 1936.

Schmid, K. A., *Geschichte der Erziehung vom Anfang an bis auf unsere Zeit*, 3 vols., Stuttgart, 1884-1892.

Schmidlin, J., *Papstgeschichte der neuesten Zeit*, t. 2. *Papsttum und Päpste gegenüber den modernen Strömungen, Pius IX und Leo XIII, 1846-1903*, München, 1934.

Schmitz, Yves, *Guillaume Ier et la Belgique*, Bruxelles: Ad. Goemaere, 1945.

Schulz, H., *Die Schulreform der Sozialdemokratie*, 2. ed., Berlin, 1919.

Simon, A., *Le Cardinal Sterckx et son Temps, 1792-1867*, 2 vols., Wetteren: Editions Scaldis, 1950.

———, *L'Église catholique et les Débuts de la Belgique indépendante*, Wetteren: Editions Scaldis, 1949.

———, *La Liberté d'Enseignement en Belgique. Essai historique*, Liège: La Pensée catholique, 1951.

Sluys, A., *Geschiedenis van het Onderwijs in de drie Graden in Belgie tijdens de Fransche Overheersching en de Regeering van Willem I*, Gent: Koninklijke Vlaamsche Academie voor Taal en Letterkunde, 1912.

Staatslexikon, 14 vols., Freiburg im Breisgau: Brockhaus, 1856-1866.

Steinmetz, Rudolf, *Englands Anteil an der Trennung der Niederlände*, Den Haag: M. Nijhoff, 1930.

Sterckx, Card., *La Constitution belge et l'Encyclique de Grégoire XVI. Deux Lettres sur nos Libertés constitutionnelles*, Malines, 1864.

Stokman, Siegfried, *De Religieuzen en de Onderwijspolitiek der Regeering in het Vereenigd Koninkrijk der Nederlanden*, 1814-1830, 's Gravenhage: Het R. K. Centraal Bureau voor Onderwijs en Opvoeding, 1935.

Terlinden, Charles, *L'Élévation d'Engelbert Sterckx au Siège épiscopal de Malines*, Extrait de La Vie Diocésaine, Louvain, 1909.

———, *Guillaume Ier, Roi des Pays-Bas, et l'Église catholique en Belgique, 1814-1830*, 2 vols., Bruxelles: A. Dewit, 1906.

Thiersch, F., *Über den gegenwärtigen Zustand des öffentlichen Unterrichts in den westlichen Staaten von Deutschland, in Holland, Frankreich und Belgien*, 3 vols., Stuttgart, 1838.

Thonissen, Jean-Joseph, *La Belgique sous le regne de Léopold Ier*, 2. ed., 3 vols., Louvain: Van Linthout & Cie, 1861.

———, *La Constitution Belge annotée*, offrant sous chaque article l'état de la Doctrine, de la Jurisprudence et de la Législation, 3. ed., Bruxelles: Christophe-Bruylant, 1879.

Troch, Aug., *Wet tot Regeling van het Lager Onderwijs en Modelreglement*, 6. ed., Lier: Van In & Cie, 1951.

Van Bemmel, Eugène, *Patria Belgica.* Encyclopédie Nationale ou Exposé méthodique de toutes les connaissances relatives à la Belgique ancienne et moderne, physique, sociale, et intellectuelle, 3 vols., Bruxelles: Bruylant-Christophe & Cie, 1873-1875.

Vanden Gheyn, Chanoine, *Le Diocèse de Gand et le premier Siècle de l'Indépendance belge*, Gand, 1932.

van der Essen, Léon, *Deux mille Ans d'Histoire.* Texte élaboré et mis au point par un groupe d'Historiens. Présentation par Léon van der Essen, Bruxelles: Éditions universitaires, 1946.

———, *La Belgique dans le Royaume des Pays-Pas, 1814-1830*, Bruxelles: La lecture au foyer, 1924.

———, *La Belgique indépendante*, Bruxelles: Éditions universitaires, 1945.

———, *A short History of Belgium*, 2. ed., Chicago: The University of Chicago Press, 1920.

———, *La Révolution belge et les Origines de notre Indépendance, 1830-1839*, Bruxelles: La Lecture au Foyer, 1927.

———, *L'Université de Louvain, 1425-1940*, Bruxelles: Éditions universitaires, 1945.

van der Smissen, E., *Léopold II et Beernaert, d'après leur Correspondance inédite*, 2 vols., Bruxelles: Ad. Goemaere, 1920.

Vandervelde, Émile, *Le Parti ouvrier belge de 1885 à 1925*, Bruxelles: L'Églantine, 1925.

van Hogendorp, Gijsbrecht, *De Ontwikkeling, 13 Dec. 1830-26 Jan. 1831*, 's Gravenhage: W. K. Mandemaker, 1830-1831.

Van Hove, A., *Commentarium Lovaniense in Codicem Iuris Canonici*, Vol. I, Tom. II, *De Legibus Ecclesiasticis*, Mechliniae-Romae: H. Dessain, 1930.

———, *Le Libéralisme et la Liberté d'Enseignement*, extrait de *La Tribune Apologétique*, Louvain, 1913, IV, 329-344, 393-404, 449-465.

———, *La Neutralité Scolaire*, Liège: La Pensée Catholique, 1927.

———, *La Séparation de l'Église et de l'État*, extrait de *La Nouvelle Revue Théologique*, 1924, LI, 425-435, 449-463, 534-553.

Van Kalken, Frans, *La Belgique contemporaine, 1780-1930.* Histoire d'une Évolution politique, Paris: Colin, 1930.

———, *Entre deux Guerres. Esquisse de la Vie politique en Belgique de 1918 à 1940*, Bruxelles: Office de Publicité, 1944.

———, *Histoire de Belgique des Origines à 1914*, Bruxelles: Office de Publicité, 1944.

———, *Histoire du Royaume des Pays-Pas et de la Révolution belge de 1830*, Bruxelles: J. Lebègue, & Cie, 1910.

van Langenhove, Fernand, *La Volonté nationale belge en 1830*, Bruxelles-Paris: G. Van Oest & Cie, 1917.

van Mol, Henri, *Manuel de Droit constitutionnel de la Belgique,* 12. ed., Liège: G. Thone, 1949.

Van Overbergh, Cyril, *Le Projet de Loi.* Ce que tout Père de famille doit savoir, Bruxelles: Comité de Propagande, 1911.

Van Overloop, Eugène, *Exposé des Motifs de la Constitution belge,* par un Docteur en Droit, Bruxelles: Goemaere, 1864.

Van Roey, Ernest, Cardinal, *Au Service de l'Église. In den Dienst van de Kerk,* 4 vols., Turnhout: Brepols, 1939-1940.

Verhaegen, Pieter, *De Schoolstrijd in Belgie,* Sottegem: Eylenbosch-Dupon, 1906.

Vermeersch, Arturus-Creusen, Josephus, *Epitome Iuris Canonici,* 3 vols., Vol. I, 6. ed., 1937; Vol. II, 6. ed., 1940; Vol. III, 5. ed., 1936; Mechliniae-Romae: H. Dessain.

Vincent, John-Vincent, Ada, *Constitution of the Kingdom of Belgium.* Translated and supplied with an Introduction and Notes. Supplement to the Annals of the American Academy of Political and Social Science, Vol. VII, n. 3, May 1896, Philadelphia: American Academy of Political Science, 1896.

Willequet, Jacques, *1830, Naissance de l'État belge,* Bruxelles: Éditions du Temple, 1950.

Woeste, Charles, *Vingt Ans de Polémique, 1865-1885,* 3 vols., Bruxelles, 1885.

———, *Échos des Luttes contemporaines, 1895-1905,* Bruxelles: Schepens & Cie, 1906.

———, *Mémoires pour servir à l'Histoire contemporaine de la Belgique,* 3 vols., Bruxelles: A. Dewit, 1927-1937.

Woywod, Stanislaus-Smith, Callistus, *A Practical Commentary on the Code of Canon Law,* 2 vols., New York: J. F. Wagner, Inc., 1948.

Periodicals

American Ecclesiastical Review, The, Vols. I-XXXII, Philadelphia, 1889-1905; from 1905: *The Ecclesiastical Review,* Vols. XXXIII-CIX, Philadelphia, 1905-1943; from 1944: *The American Ecclesiastical Review,* Washington, D. C., Vol. CX, 1944—

Apollinaris, Romae, 1928—

Catholic Historical Review, The, Washington, D. C., 1915—

Collationes Brugenses, Brugis, 1896—

Collationes Gandavenses, Gandae, 1909—

Collationes Namurcenses, Namurci, 1901—

Collationes Tornacenses, Tornaci, 1853—

Collectanea Mechliniensia, Mechliniae, 1927—

C.O.V.-Leidersblad, Rillaar, 1948—

Documentation catholique, La, Paris, 1919—

Enseignement libre, L', Bruxelles, 1940—

Ephemerides Theologicae Lovanienses, Louvain, 1924—
Jurist, The, Washington, D. C., 1941—
Monitore Ecclesiastico, Il, Roma, 1876-1948.
Ons Geloof, Antwerpen, 1911—
Osservatore Romano, L', Roma, 1861-1929; Città del Vaticano, 1929—
Periodica de Re Canonica et Morali utilia praesertim Religiosis et Missionariis, 7 vols., Brugis, 1920-1927; from 1927: *Periodica de Re Morali, Canonica, Liturgica,* Brugis, 1927-1936, et Romae, 1937—
Revue d' Histoire ecclésiastique, Louvain, 1905—
Revue ecclesiastique de Liège, Liège, 1908—

ABBREVIATIONS

AAS—*Acta Apostolicae Sedis*
ASS—*Acta Sanctae Sedis*
Enchiridion—Denzinger-Bannwart-Umberg, *Enchiridion Symbolorum* . . .
Fontes—Codicis Iuris Canonici Fontes
S.C.C.—Sacra Congregatio Concilii
S.C. de Prop. Fide—Sacra Congregatio de Propaganda Fide
S.C. Ep. et Reg.—Sacra Congregatio Episcoporum et Regularium
S.C.S. Off.—Suprema Congregatio Sancti Officii

ALPHABETICAL INDEX

Adoptable schools, 109
Adopted schools, 103
  authority over, 105
  building of, 106
  curriculum of, 107
  financial setup of, 108
  free admission to, 108
  inspection of, 107
  medical inspection of, 107
  teachers in, 106, 110
Adoption of schools, 103
  conditions of, 106-109
  contract of, 104
  and confessional schools, 107
  duration of, 109
  meaning of, 104
  judgment on the, 110-111, 122
  and local autonomy, 105
  parties involved in the, 104
  and rights of minorities, 107
Albert I, 94
Anti-Catholic schools, 27
  attendance at, 32
Anti-Clericalism, 48
Antwerp, 37
Aquinas, St. Thomas, 4
Artois, 37
Assembly of prominent Citizens, 40
Austria, 37, 38
Autonomy, Local, 47, 67, 91, 105, 109, 120
  and educational rights of parents, 23

Baptism, 3, 6, 10, 11, 25
Belgium,
  dioceses of, 36
  history of, 36
  population and territory of, 37
  provinces of, 37
Bishops (see also *Hierarchy* and *Ordinaries*), 13
Bonaparte, 38, 47
Books,
  authorization of, 46
  Church control of, 13, 15, 17
Bourbons, 51
British policy, 38
Bruges, 36
Brussels, 51
  Congress of, 75, 76
  University of, 67
Building, School, 103, 106
Burgundy, 37, 39
  Dukes of, 37

Caesar, Julius, 36
Canon Law, Code of, 1, 11, 12, 15, 17, 18, 27, 30, 31, 33, 35
Carton de Wiart, 115
Catechetics, 34
Catholic Action, 19
Catholic Party, 75, 95
Catholic Schools (see also *Confessional schools*), 8
  attendance at, 26
  establishment of, 17
    obligation of, 18
    right of the Church to, 17
  management of, 13
  meaning of, 8, 26
  necessity of, 17, 18, 26
  organization of, 84
  secular education in, 33
Catholic School System, 9, 13, 33
  necessity of, 18
Central government,
  and adoption of schools, 105
  Belgian, 63
  Dutch, 45
Certificate of studies, 103, 106
Christ (see also *God*), 2, 3, 6, 25, 28
Church, 3
  indirect authority, 16
  and compulsory school attendance, 21
  and Belgian Constitution, 54
  educational duties and rights, 5, 9
  alleged intolerance, 6
  a moral person, 9
  the representative of the families, 5, 7, 9
  right of educating clergy, 10
  right of forming its members, 10
  right of having its own schools, 17
  right of supervision over all schools, 12, 17, 118, 121
  historical right to teach, 9, 25

and Belgian school legislation, 115, 121
schools of the, 8
a necessary society, 3, 9
a perfect society, 3, 10
a supernatural society, 3, 24
the divinely appointed teacher, 1, 10, 28
Church schools (see *Confessional* and *Denominational schools*)
Civic duties, Training for, 21
Civic education, 20
and rights of parents, 20
in confessional schools, 25, 29
Civil public schools, 8, 103
authority of Church over, 14, 17, 34
religious instruction in, 23
justification of, 22
Civil society (see *State*)
Clergy (see also *Priests, Seminaries*)
education of, 10, 58
and Belgian revolution, 50
teachers of religion, 116
Committees, School, 84
Committees of supervision,
Dutch, 45, 47
Communal law, 62
and school legislation, 103
Communal schools, 103
religious instruction in, 115
Communes, Independent, 37
Compromise, Law of, 62
application of, 73
contents of, 69
judgment on, 69, 83
justification of, 65
passing of, 69
revision of, 76
Compulsory education,
general principle of, 20
in Belgian legislation,
general rule, 100
and freedom of instruction, 101
suspension of obligation, 10
Concordat of 1827, 48
Confessional schools (see also *Catholic schools*), 8, 27
common in 19th century, 46
public funds for, 22, 111
public order and, 23
required by parents, 23
legal status of, 103
Congo, Belgian, 38
Constitution,
Belgian, 37, 48
Church-State relations in, 54
contents of, 53
and education, 56
and modern freedoms, 52, 54
and Hierarchy, 56
importance of, 53
and Holy See, 55
Dutch, 40
Control of schools
(see *Inspection*)
Councils, 2
Curriculum,
of adoptable schools, 109
of adopted schools, 103
of civil public schools, 16, 28, 115

de Broglie, 40, 41
de Broqueville, 95, 99
de Burlet, 91
Dechamps, 70
Dechamps, Cardinal, 76
Declaration of the Rights of Man and Citizens, 49
de Méan, 41, 57
de Mérode, 70
Denominational schools
(see *Confessional schools*)
de Nothomb, 65, 70, 71
de Potter, 49
Destrée, 115
Dioceses, Belgian, 36
Diploma
(see *Certificate of studies*)
Diplomats,
training of, 21
Discrimination, 109, 112, 115
District Inspector, 43, 45
Divini illius Magistri, 1, 2, 16
and compulsory instruction, 21
and nature of schools, 7, 24
and philosophy of education, 25
and rights of Church, 16
and rights of Parents, 4
and rights of State, 16, 19
summary of, 2
and support of schools, 18
Doctrinal Decision, 41
Dutch regime, 37, 38
(see also *United Kingdom* and *William I*)

East-Flanders, 37
Ecclesiastical public schools
(see *Confessional schools*)
Educational activities, 22
Elementary schools, 8
necessity of, 6

England, 38
(see also *British policy*)
Europe, 37, 38, 39, 46, 53

Faithful, Duties of, 18
Family (see also *Parents*), 3
and Church authority, 11
duties and rights of the, 4, 6
its rights protected by Church, 6
its rights violated by States, 5, 6
and school, 7
as a society, 3
Féron, 98
Feudalism, 36
Financial support
(see *Funds*)
Flanders, 37
France, 37
Freedom of assembly, 52
Freedom of Association, 52
Freedom of instruction, 52
abuses of, 61
a consequence of freedom of religion, 57
in the Belgian Constitution, 52, 58
and school legislation, 66
Freedom of press, 49, 52
Freedom of religion, 49
in the Belgian Constitution, 52
and freedom of instruction, 52, 57
Freemasons, 28, 64, 76, 84, 89
and Church, 64
Fundamental Law, Dutch, 40
and Belgian Hierarchy, 41
Funds, Public (see also *School aid*)
for denominational schools, 22, 111

Gallia Belgica, 36
General Assembly for Primary Instruction, 45
Germany, 38, 99
God (see also *Christ*), 2, 3, 4, 6, 75
Government employees,
training of, 21
Grace, 3, 10
Gregory XVI, Pope, 56
Ghent, 36, 40, 41

Hainaut, 37
Heretical schools, 28
(see also *Confessional schools*)
Hierarchy (see also *Bishops and Ordinary*), Belgian,
and the Belgian Constitution, 53
Doctrinal Decision of the, 41
and Freemasons, 64
and Dutch Fundamental Law, 41, 47
and Law of Compromise, 70
and Law of Misfortune, 76, 78, 80, 82
and Revolution of 1830, 17
and civil public schools, 115
and present school system, 119
and *Union of the Opposition*, 49
and William I, 40
Holland (see *Dutch Regime*)
Higher learning, Schools of, 9
Holy Office, 28, 34
Holy See,
and attendance at non-Catholic institutions, 31
diplomatic relations with, 86, 88
and Belgian Constitution, 53
and Freemasons, 64
and Belgian School Fight, 86
and *Union of the Opposition*, 49
and William I, 41, 48
Huysmans, 115, 121

Independent schools, 102
Indifferentism, 28, 29
Inspection,
of religious instruction, 15, 118
of schools,
by Church, 15, 84, 115, 118
by State, 19, 107
under Dutch regime, 43
Intermediate schools, 9

Jacobs, 89
Jesus (see *Christ*)
Jews,
and Belgian Constitution, 54
and civil public schools, 115
Joseph II, 47
Justice, Distributive, 22
and public funds for schools, 22
and school aid, 114

King,
Belgian (see also *Albert I*, and *Leopold II*)
legal position of, 63
and school aid, 114
Dutch, 45 (see also *William I*)

Lamennais, 49
Law,
of compromise, 62
of misfortune, 75
of restoration, 88
of reconciliation, 96

Lawyers, Training of, 21
Lay schools, 27
  (see also *Neutral schools*)
Lebeau, 64
Leftist cartel, 94
Legislation, School,
  Belgian (see *Law*)
  Dutch, 43
Leo XII, Pope, 64
Leo XIII, Pope,
  and education, 5, 86
  and socialism, 5
  and Belgian Constitution, 55
Leopold II, 89, 91
Liberalism, Theory of, 30
  and Belgian Constitution, 55
  and the Church, 55
Liberals, Belgian, 48
  and Catholic religion, 48
  and Belgian Revolution, 48
  and school laws, 59, 94
Libraries, 20
License, Teaching, 43
Liège, 36, 37, 50
Limburg, 37
London, Treaties of, 63
Lotteries, 109
Louvain, University of, 64, 67
Low Countries, 38
Luxemburg, 37

Majority, Parliamentary, 77
Malines, 36, 56
  Congresses of, 75
Malou, 89
Man, Conception of, 3, 24, 33
Masons (see *Freemasons*)
Materne, Saint, 36
Medical inspection, 107, 113
Mercier, Cardinal, 96, 99
Merovingian Kings, 36
Metternich, 39
Meuse, 38
Middle ages, 37
Military training, 21
Minorities, Rights of the,
  and adoption of schools, 105
  and Catholic majority, 117
  and reconciliation laws, 97
  respect for, 6, 117
  and restoration law, 90
  and school aid, 114
  in neutral schools, 27
  and system of school coupon, 93
Misfortune, Law of, 75
  (see also *School Fight*)
  condemnation of, 77, 79
  consequences of, 80
  and Freemasons, 76
  supreme jurisdiction of the government under the, 78
  judgment on the, 82
  and Leopold II, 79
  passing of, 79
  and civic responsibilities of the individual, 79
  revocation of, 88
  secularization of education through the, 77
Mixed schools, 8, 23, 34, 48
  attendance at, 29, 32
  under Dutch rule, 46
Monopoly, School,
  by the Church, 18, 59
  by the State, 7
    and Belgian Constitution, 59
    under Dutch rule, 42
Moral persons,
  Rights of, 9
Morality, Norm of, 3, 24
Museums, 20

Namur, 36, 37
Napoleon, 38, 47
Nassau, 38
National Congress, 52
  and freedom of instruction, 57
National Union, Government of, 99
Natural order, 3, 4, 9
Naturalism, Theory of, 30
Neglect, Parental, 20
Neutral schools, 8, 23, 28, 34, 48
  attendance at, 28, 32
  differing from lay schools, 27
  under Dutch rule, 46
Neutrality, Educational, 23, 27
Non-Catholic schools,
  attendance at, 27
    prohibition, 27
      extent of, 27
      reasons for, 30
    tolerance, 31
      circumstances for, 32
      precautions, 34
    penalties, 33, 34
Normal schools, 21
North Sea, 38

Obligatory schools, 9
Official schools, 103
  (see *Civil public schools* and *Communal schools*)

Officials, Training of, 21
Optional schools, 9
Orange, Prince of, 38
(see *William I*)
Ordinary, Local,
(see also *Bishops* and *Hierarchy*)
right of inspection of, 15
permitting non-Catholic schools, 31
educational duties of, 18

Pagan schools, 28, 33
(see also *Confessional schools*)
Parents (see also *Family*)
duties and rights of, 4, 34, 35, 81, 120
and public funds for schools, 22
and modern philosophy, 24
and compulsory school attendance, 20, 34, 101
and school legislation, 5, 120
representatives of Church, 11, 13, 14
delegating the Church, 5, 9, 11
Paris, 38
Parochial schools,
(see *Confessional schools*)
Pax Romana, 36
Penalties, 33, 34
Petitions,
to Dutch government, 50
to Belgian government, 79
right of, 57
Philip the Good, 37
Philosophical College, 42
Philosophy of education,
Christian, 24
pagan, 24
Physicians, Training of, 21
Pius XI, Pope,
(see *Divini illius Magistri*)
Pope, Authority of the, 13
Poullet, 95, 96, 97
Practical Instructions, 80
Preaching, 1
Priests, Duties of, 18, 81
(see also *Clergy* and *Seminaries*)
Primary schools, 8
Private schools, 8, 13, 17, 44
(see also *Adoptable schools*)
authority over, 13
Dutch, 44
Protestants, 46 (see also *Minorities*)
and Belgian Constitution, 54
and civil public schools, 115
Provincial Committee of Inspectors,
Dutch, 44
Provincial Law, 62
Provisional Government, 51
Prussia, 38
Public ecclesiastical Law, 3
Public funds, 22, 111
Public Instruction, Ministry of,
Public order, 20
and confessional schools, 25
Public professions, Training for, 21
Public schools, 8
(see also *Civil public schools* and *Confessional schools*)

Reconciliation, Laws of
contents of, the, 97
passing of the, 97
Regulations, School,
Belgian, 103
Dutch, 45
Religious instruction in schools,
under direction of Church, 13
excluded under Dutch regime, 46
importance of, 25
and Belgian legislation,
in adoptable schools, 109
in adopted schools, 103
in civil public schools, 23, 115
consequences of, 117
dispensation from, 117
without discrimination, 115
inspection of, 118
organization of, 116
principle of, 116
Religious schools, 8, 23
Religious teachers,
discrimination against, 112
Restoration Laws,
contents of, 88, 90
and Freemasons, 89
and Leopold II, 89
meaning of, 90
passing of, 88, 90
Revolution,
Belgian, 37, 47, 51
of the Three Glorious Days, 51
French, 38
Rhine, 38
Rogier, 75
Ruanda-Urundi, 38
Royal Message, 51
Russia, 38

Sacraments, 10
Sanctions, 33, 34
Scheldt, 38
Schismatic schools, 28
(see also *Confessional schools*)

Schollaert, 91, 96
School,
  classifications, 7
  pagan conception of, 24
  confessional, 8
  definition of, 7
  denominational, 8
  elementary, 8
  and family, 7
  intermediate, 9
  of higher learning, 9
  mixed, 8
  neutral, 8
  obligatory, 9
  optional, 9
  origin and nature of, 7, 24
  private, 8
  public, 8
  religious, 8
  supervised by Church, 4
School aid, 114 (see also *Funds*)
School Coupon, System of the, 93
School Fight (see also *Misfortune*)
  and Hierarchy, 80
  preparation of, 80
  principles of, 80
  methods of, 80, 84
  economical side of, 86
  success of, 85
  solution of, 88
School Funds (see *Funds*)
School Inquiry, 86
School Legislation (see *Law*)
School Problem, 7
School System, 7, 9
Sciences, Teaching of, 16
Secondary schools, 9
Secular education, 1, 33
Secularization of schools, 77
Secret Societies, 64
Seminaries (see also *Clergy*)
  and Belgian Constitution, 58, 59
  right to found, 10
  under Dutch rule, 42
  and military service, 64
Socialism, 5
Socialists, 97
Spaak, 121
Spanish rule, 37
State, 3
  duties and rights of the, 16, 19, 20, 122
    Belgian Constitution and, 10
    parental rights and, 4, 5, 19
    Church rights and, 16
  a necessary society, 3, 9
  a perfect society, 3, 10
Sterckx, Cardinal,
  and Belgian Constitution, 56
  and school law of 1942, 65, 72, 76, 83
Subsidies (see *Funds*)
Subsidized Liberty, System of, 122
Subsidized schools (see *Adoptable* and *Adopted schools*)
Supernatural order, 3, 10
Supervision (see *Inspection*)
Surlet de Chokier, 57

Taxation (see *Funds*)
Teachers,
  of religion, 13, 17
  religious, 112
  in adopted schools, 106
    appointment of, 107
    qualifications of, 106
    salaries of, 110
  in civil public schools, 81
    Church authority over, 17, 34
  in private schools, 13
    Church authority over, 13
  training of, 21
Thames, 38
Tongeren, 36
Tournai, 36
Training schools, 21
Trent, Council of, 42

Union of the Opposition, 49, 51, 59, 64
United Kingdom, 39 (see also *Dutch regime* and *William I*)
United States, 53
Universities, 9, 67

Van de Walle, 98
Van Humbeeck, 75, 87
Van Roey, Cardinal, 119
Veydt, 71
Vienna, Congress of, 38
Visitation of Schools, (see *Inspection*)

Waterloo, 38
West-Flanders, 37
William I, 38
  and Belgian grievances, 48
  and Belgian Hierarchy, 41
  and Holy See, 41, 48
  and Liberals, 48
  educational policy of, 42
Woeste, 82, 89, 94
World War I, 99
World War II, 121

BIOGRAPHICAL NOTE

GOMMAR ALBERT LEO JULIAAN DE PAUW was born on October 11, 1918, in Stekene (East-Flanders, Belgium). At the age of seventeen he graduated *magna cum laude* from the Catholic College of Saint Nicholas-Waas, whereupon he entered the diocesan Seminary of Ghent for his philosophical and theological studies. At the outbreak of World-War II he participated with the ninth Belgian Infantry Regiment in the campaigns of Belgium, Holland, and France, where at the battle of Dunkirk he was taken prisoner. After his escape from prison-camp he returned to the Seminary. Upon the completion of his theological studies he was, by indult of the Holy See, ordained to the priesthood at the age of twenty-three. After a temporary assignment as subregent and professor at Saint Nicholas College, he was sent for three years of post-graduate studies to the Catholic University of Louvain. Besides the regular course of study for the Doctorate in Canon Law he also followed there a three-year course in Moral Theology and in Church History, and a one-year course in International Law and in Archeology. With the Belgian Underground Army and the First Free Polish Armored Division he took part in the liberation of Northern Belgium and Southern Holland in 1944 and 1945. While continuing research work in the field of European Church-State relations he was appointed assistant pastor and moderator of the Catholic Workers' Organization. In 1949 he came to the United States, where the De Pauws had been among the first settlers of the seventeenth century in New York. For two years he was assistant pastor in New York City. During the academic year 1951-1952 he came to the School of Canon Law of the Catholic University of America where, after a year of final research work, he presented this dissertation for a doctoral degree.

CANON LAW STUDIES*

327. KOESLER, REV. LEO J., O.S.B., J.C.L., *Entrance into the Novitiate by Clerics in Major Orders (Canon 542, 2°).*
328. MCFARLAND, REV. NORMAN E., J.C.L., *Essential Conditions and Sufficient Signs of Vocation to the Religious Life.*
329. WIEST, REV. DONALD HERMAN, O.F.M.CAP., S.T.B., J.C.L., *The Precensorship of Books.*
330. DE WITT, REV. MAX GEORGE, A.B., J.C.L., *The Cessation of Delegated Power.*
331. MATHIS, REV. MARCIAN JOHN, O.F.M., J.C.L., *The Constitution and Supreme Administration of Regional Seminaries Subject to the Sacred Congregation for the Propagation of the Faith in China.*
332. SCHORR, REV. GEORGE F., A.B., J.C.L., *The Law of the Celebret.*
333. SHEEHY, REV. ROBERT FRANCIS, A.B., J.C.L., *The Sacred Congregation of the Sacraments: Its Competence in the Roman Curia.*
334. SHIELDS, REV. JOSEPH A., A.B., J.C.L., *Deprivation of the Clerical Garb.*
335. URICHECK, REV. GEORGE EDWARD, A.B., J.C.L., *De forma celebrationis matrimomii in Ecclesiis Orientalibus* ante Motu Proprio *Crebrae Allatae* et post.

*For a complete list of the available numbers of this series apply to the Catholic University of America Press, 620 Michigan Avenue, N.E., Washington 17, D. C.

www.ingramcontent.com/pod-product-compliance
Lightning Source LLC
LaVergne TN
LVHW050223080826
844660LV00012B/457
* 9 7 8 0 8 1 3 2 2 5 0 6 7 *